IMAGES
of America

THE PORT
OF HOUSTON

ON THE COVER: The Turning Basin is the heart of the Port of Houston. Break-bulk cargo ships line the docks in 1956. That year, *Ideal-X* arrived at the port carrying the first load of shipping containers, a cargo that would forever change the Port of Houston and the ships that used it. (Courtesy University of Houston Digital Archive Library.)

IMAGES
of America

THE PORT OF HOUSTON

Mark Lardas

ARCADIA
PUBLISHING

Copyright © 2013 by Mark Lardas
ISBN 9781531675516

Published by Arcadia Publishing
Charleston, South Carolina

Library of Congress Control Number: 2013938513

For all general information, please contact Arcadia Publishing:
Telephone 843-853-2070
Fax 843-853-0044
E-mail sales@arcadiapublishing.com
For customer service and orders:
Toll-Free 1-888-313-2665

Visit us on the Internet at www.arcadiapublishing.com

To Janet: You have kept me sane and centered for nearly 40 years.

Contents

Foreword		6
Acknowledgments		7
1.	A Visit to the Port	9
2.	The Early Years	25
3.	A Seaport Is Born	39
4.	The Opening Years	51
5.	Depression and War	65
6.	The Brawny Years	77
7.	The Container Revolution	91
8.	Expansion and Growth	103
9.	A 21st-Century Port	115
Bibliography		127

FOREWORD

Houston's port has been cited as "irreplaceable" by Colliers International, as "the defining engine of our economy and culture" by *Cite* magazine, and as the generator of more than one million jobs and $180 billion of regional economic activity by Martin Associates. In 2014, the port will celebrate 100 years of service as the region's catalyst for economic growth. Throughout the world, the Port of Houston is recognized as the most significant factor in Houston's status as a foremost international-trade and energy center.

Inspired by the rich history of the port and its impact on the nation's fourth-largest city, author Mark Lardas's *The Port of Houston* captures the essence of the port before and since the deepwater channel opened in 1914. Beginning with steamboat trade in the 1830s, followed by the unyielding persistence of city leaders, federal funding was secured by congressman Tom Ball for the deepening and widening of the Houston Ship Channel in 1909. The completion of the channel, coupled with the establishment of Houston as the railroad center of the South and the booming cotton, lumber, and petroleum industries, earned the city the designation "Where 17 Railroads Meet the Sea." The port was a major factor in Houston's phenomenal growth of the 1920s, adding more than 50 businesses that located along the channel, and it continues to lead economic development today, generating more than one million jobs and $178 billion of economic development across the state. Lardas's story substantiates the profound observation made by Will Rogers: "Houston dared to dig a ditch, and brought the sea to its door."

Surprisingly, the worldwide acclaim for the Port of Houston and the maritime industry as the leading economic engine for the region is largely unrecognized by the residents it serves. To that end, the Houston Maritime Museum was founded in 2000 to serve as a beacon of education and appreciation for the wonder and influence of maritime history and the regional marine industry. The museum features hundreds of exceptional ship models and navigational instruments that illustrate the story of navigation from the age of exploration to today. Presently located in the Houston Museum District, the museum is planning a move to the Sam Houston Pavilion, located at the Turning Basin on the Port of Houston, as part of the 100th-anniversary celebration. This 25,000-square-foot, world-class maritime museum will feature a 110-foot scaled model of the Houston Ship Channel with recognition of all the businesses that surround it.

The Port of Houston will enlighten readers about the maritime world and its extraordinary impact on the development of the region and the daily lives of more than six million residents. Delve into the vision of the city's forefathers and the determination for prosperity that led to the observation that "Houston is the town that built the port that built the city!"

—Diane Lipton
Executive Director, Houston Maritime Museum
www.houstonmaritimemuseum.org

ACKNOWLEDGMENTS

No book is the product of a single author. Many folks helped me as I wrote and assembled this volume, and I would especially like to note those mentioned here.

The Houston Maritime Museum provided tremendous support for this project. Special thanks have to go to former director John Kendall and current director Diane Lipton, as well as to Mary Barnes and Heather Schiappa. Thanks also go to Burt Reckles, a docent at the Houston Maritime Museum as well as a friend and fellow ship modeler.

The Port of Houston Authority also provided invaluable support, especially Leslie Herbst, Phil Hensel, and Deya Martinez. Without them, I would not have found many of the most striking images in this book.

My deep gratitude goes to Michele Reilly, head of digital services at the University of Houston. She went above and beyond the call of duty to help me acquire images from the university's digital archives. It is worth a visit at http://digital.lib.uh.edu/.

Special thanks go to Robert Thompson of the Houston Pilots Association. He made an effort to allow me to accompany him as he piloted a ship through the Houston Ship Channel, but circumstances made it impossible to take up his offer.

I would also like to thank Laura Bruns, my acquisitions editor at Arcadia Publishing, for her assistance.

Finally, thanks go to my wife, Janet, for her support during this project.

The following abbreviations indicate the sources of the images used in this volume:
AC—author's collection
HMM—Houston Maritime Museum
LOC—Library of Congress
NARA—National Archives
NASA—National Aerospace and Space Administration
POHA—Port of Houston Authority
UHDL—University of Houston Digital Archive Library
USACOE—US Army Corps of Engineers

As the port finishes its first century as a deepwater seaport, interest in its history and heritage has grown. The port is responding to that interest by supporting the Houston Maritime Museum in a move to a new building at the port. (AP.)

One

A Visit to the Port

Take a visit to the Port of Houston. Many visitors seeking to see the port stop off at Allen's Landing first. The Allen brothers were said to have founded Houston there, taking a steamboat up Buffalo Bayou as far as it would go. Today, Allen's Landing is a park in Houston's downtown. It does not match expectations of what a seaport should look like. Today, it cannot be seen as a place that river steamboats could have reached, much less oceangoing ships. The bayou there seems too narrow for a barge—or maybe even a canoe.

Many are curious about the Port of Houston, which is a major part of the city's identity. Ask anyone to tell two things about Houston. Most will say that it is America's space city and a seaport, or that it is the oil capital of the United States and a seaport.

Visitors can tour the port aboard the *Sam Houston*, for those curiosity move beyond Allen's Landing. The tours are free, take 90 minutes, and depart every day but Monday. It is another opportunity to learn a little about the port.

Visitors must show picture identification to enter the port when they arrive at the gate. Since 9/11, the Department of Homeland Security requires this. They are directed to a parking lot next to a pavilion marking the *Sam Houston*'s dock. *Sam Houston* is all white and 95 feet long, with a two-level deckhouse set jauntily amidships. It reminds many of a plastic toy boat owned in childhood. Perhaps that is not so strange. *Sam Houston* is older than many realize, launched in 1957. A toy maker might easily have modeled a childhood toy on a ship like *Sam Houston*.

When visitors explore the ship, they will discover plenty of space for the people taking most tours. A full house will run 80 to 100 people, something that usually happens on weekends. The boat has an air-conditioned lounge, which is really nice on a summer day. Really fortunate visitors take the trip on a warm winter's day, when it is comfortable standing on deck, outside the lounge, so the port can easily been viewed

In the lounge, a big mural showing a stylized view of the Port of Houston was placed. Burly men with forklifts move pallets of cargo. Brawny longshoremen load sacks, bales, and forty-gallon drums onto other pallets to be lifted into the holds of ships. The ships have graceful clipper bows, a deckhouse and smokestack amidships, and booms and masts in front of and behind the central island. This was what the port looked like back when the Sam Houston was launched, in the middle of the 20th century.

The big diesel engines of the Sam Houston come to life. Visitors feel the vibration on the deck through their shoes. The ship moves away from the dock. Until then, visitors are confined to the lounge.

Those exiting the lounge then to look at the harbor first notice three large ships, painted medium gray. Other ships are colorful—in reds, oranges, black, and white. These three are drab. Even their names are painted in a dull black: *Cape Taylor* on one, *Cape Texas* on a second, and *Cape Trinity* on the third. Most of the other ships seen are hives of activity. These three are quiet, seemingly forgotten. They look like naval ships, despite the Port of Houston being a commercial port. They are Ready Reserve Force fleet ships that support the United States military. These roll-on/roll-off ships are used to move army vehicles, if tanks and other military vehicles at Fort Hood, Texas, need to be moved to some trouble spot. These ships look different than the ones in the mural. In fact, most ships look different. The deckhouses and smokestacks are at the back. The booms and masts are missing. The hulls seem blunter. Many ships are piled up with shipping containers, often piled six high above the deck. Visitors can only guess how many more are hidden within the hull.

Now, the *Sam Houston* has turned 180 degrees and is cruising downstream, heading towards Galveston Bay. Literature on board calls this area the Turning Basin. It is a notch in Buffalo Bayou. Its purpose is to give ships a place to turn, so they can point their bows back downstream. It would be hard to have to back a ship the length of the bayou, until it reached Galveston Bay. Thoughtful visitors often wonder if a ship could turn in Galveston Bay. Isn't it too shallow for deep-draft ships?

Now, *Sam Houston* is moving downstream. The term *bayou* brings the image of narrow, winding waterways choked with trees growing in shallow, muddy water and fallen timber. While the water is muddy, Buffalo Bayou looks like a river. It is not all that wide right here, maybe 500 feet, but at this spot it seems fairly straight, with gentle curves. What is striking is how crowded it seems—not the center channel, in which the *Sam Houston* cruises, but along and on the banks.

As *Sam Houston* motors downstream, it passes moored seagoing vessels painted in bright primary colors. As it passes, their names and nationalities are announced over *Sam Houston's* public-address system. Some look new, others look rusty. The ribs can be seen on a few, the hull battered in between frames, like a starved horse.

All have slab-sided full hulls, with deck structures fore and aft. Casual visitors might assume they are different types of vessels, but few can really tell. Several have warnings against smoking. Are these tankers of some kind? A few have big hemispheres on their decks, looking like the tops of gas storage tanks. Others have wide hatches that run the width of the ship. One of these is partly filled with shipping containers. It must be a container ship.

More numerous are the smaller vessels filling the channel: barges and tugs. Most are tied up along the bank. *Sam Houston* passes one barge being loaded with what a casual visitor would initially assume is bark mulch. Only after the PA announces *Sam Houston* is passing a scrap metal facility do passengers realize their perception of scale is off. The cargo is not bark mulch. It is scrap iron, rusty brown.

So it goes, down the channel and back. The boat passes shore facilities. Unless there is a sign by the bank identifying it, or the place is named over the PA system when it is passed, the average tourist has no idea what they are. Even Brady's Landing, a popular restaurant on the Houston Ship Channel at which many have eaten, would have passed unrecognized if not pointed out.

As *Sam Houston* returns to the dock, casual tourists cannot help thinking about what they saw. Despite seeing a lot, a big question remains unanswered. While it seems to work, Houston still seems like an odd place for the nation's second-largest seaport. So, what is the story? How did it get where it is and why?

The inspection boat *Sam Houston* rests at its dock. This diesel-powered vessel can carry 100 passengers and is used to conduct twice-daily tours of the Port of Houston. (AP.)

This is one of the petroleum-storage facilities that line the Houston Ship Channel and is one of the first things passed in the Port of Houston tour. (AP.)

Three Ready Reserve Fleet ships—*Cape Trinity, Cape Taylor,* and *Cape Texas*—call the Port of Houston home. They are roll-on/roll-off vessels intended to transport military vehicles, including tanks, in the event of a national emergency. (AP.)

The tug *Harris II* sits tied up at the Long Reach docks. The Long Reach docks are at the Turning Basin, for many years the heart of the port. Built in 1997, *Harris II* is owned by the Bay Houston Towing Company of Houston, Texas, founded in 1875. (AP.)

Bulk carrier *Glorious Saiki* awaits cargo in the Port of Houston. Panamanian registered, it displaces 37,000 deadweight tons. (AP.)

This barge is being loaded with scrap metal from a facility on the south side of Buffalo Bayou. (AP.)

A Houston landmark, Brady's Landing restaurant is located at the Turning Basin and offers diners a view of the port as they eat. (AP.)

The *Ray Stoker Jr.* is one of the ferries carrying vehicles between the Bolivar Peninsula and Galveston. Here, it is in Houston awaiting maintenance at one of the shipyards at the port. (AP.)

This gantry for handling shipping containers can transfer containers from truck trailers, railcars, or ships. Houston was one of the world's earliest container ports. (AP.)

The Interstate 610 Sidney Sherman Bridge, as seen from the Houston Ship Channel, opened in 1973. It is one of the most noticeable landmarks on the channel. (AP.)

The bridge normally has a 135-foot clearance, but hurricane storm surge can alter that. These height markers advise pilots as to the clearance available to a ship. (AP.)

Appearing like a clutch of giant eggs in a tidal nest, these tanks hold natural gas in a facility on the Houston Ship Channel just east of the Sidney Sherman Bridge. (AP.)

Petrochemicals have been a major industry in Houston and the Galveston Bay area since the early years of the 20th century. This is one of the older facilities on the Houston Ship Channel (AP.)

This is another of the many petrochemical plants that line the Houston Ship Channel. The Port of Houston is home to a $15 billion petrochemical complex, (AP.)

The *Pine 2* is a 34,000-deadweight-ton container ship. In this image, it sits partly loaded in at the Woodhouse Terminal on the Houston Ship Channel. (AP.)

Grain has always been a major cargo for the Port of Houston. Of the several grain elevators on the Houston Ship Channel, this is one of the largest. (AP.)

The pusher tug pictured here, the *Michael A. Duhon,* is docked on the channel. Registered in Louisiana, it is typical of today's tug fleet. (AP.)

Histria Coral is an oil tanker registered in Malta. Launched in 2006, it is typical of the tankers that use the Port of Houston to unload and receive cargoes. (AP.)

Gas Fortune carries liquefied petroleum gas (LPG). Moored at a private terminal in the Houston Ship Channel, it is riding high in the water after discharging its cargo. (AP.)

This is the United States Gypsum Company facility on the Houston Ship Channel in Galena Park, Texas. United States Gypsum is one of the major manufacturers of drywall in the country. (AP.)

A Coast Guard patrol boat passes the *Sam Houston*. Port security has become a major concern since the attacks of September 11, 2001, and the Coast Guard plays an active role in keeping the Port of Houston safe. (AP.)

The Houston Lighting & Power deepwater electrical-power-generation plant was built in 1923, in part to provide power to Houston Ship Channel industries. It is still a prominent sight on the port tour. (AP.)

Houston Refining (formerly known as Lyondell-Citgo Refining) is one of the oil refineries on the Houston Ship Channel that can be viewed from the Houston port tour. (AP.)

Far from its home port of New York City, the tug *Timothy L. Reinauer* delivers its barge cargo to the Port of Houston. (AP.)

The turnaround point on the Port of Houston tour marks the furthest downstream *Sam Houston* takes its passengers. From here, the Houston Ship Channel winds among petrochemical plants, past the San Jacinto Monument, and through the Morgan's Point cut to Galveston Bay. (AP.)

Two

THE EARLY YEARS

Throughout its history, Houston and its port have been at the intersection of technology and geography. Their combined growth and success were due as much to transportation technology as to location. Buffalo Bayou is not a major Texas river, but it was perfectly located during an era in which goods traveled by wagon or boat. Buffalo Bayou was a waterborne shortcut from the agricultural heart of Texas to Galveston, Texas's best seaport in the early 19th century.

Galveston was then the only sheltered port on the Texas coast. The others were open roadsteads or required ships to anchor offshore and transfer cargoes in small boats. Galveston Bay offered a deepwater route to the sheltered north side of Galveston Island. Before the 1830s, Galveston had been of limited use as a port as a wind for entry would block departure for a purely sail-powered ship.

Steam power fixed that. Steam tugs could move sailing vessels against the wind, and steamboats could travel Texas's narrow rivers, transforming them into freight expressways. Texas became accessible—and attractive—to investors and immigrants.

Two brothers from New York City, Augustus Chapman Allen and John Kirby Allen, recognized this opportunity. Land speculators, they wanted to found their own city, and Buffalo Bayou drew their attention. The Allen brothers were not the first to spot the Bayou's advantages; even before their arrival, developers had already established New Washington, Powhattan, and Harrisburg on Buffalo Bayou.

Harrisburg, the farthest upstream, was considered head of navigation of Buffalo Bayou. (It is located near the modern port's Turning Basin.) The Allens attempted to purchase Harrisburg, but title was clouded. Instead, the brothers picked a site five miles upstream, where White Oak Bayou met Buffalo Bayou. Declaring it the true head of navigation, they purchased the land in 1836 and platted a city on the south bank of Buffalo Bayou.

The Allen brothers proved cannier marketers than their competitors. They advertised widely and named their town after Gen. Sam Houston, hero of the Texas Revolution. The Allens convinced the government of the new Republic of Texas to use Houston as the national capital, providing the new city with instant credibility.

That credibility would fade if the Allens failed to prove that Houston was, as advertised, a port. In 1837, they hired the steamboat *Laura* to take a load of investors and potential investors to the lots purchased in Houston. The 85-foot-long *Laura* was then the smallest steamboat on Texas waters and made an easy passage to Harrisburg. It spent an additional three days traveling the remaining five miles to the Allens' new town (progress was delayed by obstacles in the bayou).

Regardless, on January 22, 1836, *Laura* tied up at a landing somewhat near the present-day Houston riverfront, today called Allens' Landing. Houston had indeed proved a port. Soon, other steamboats came visiting.

Houston's limitation as a port was demonstrated in June 1837, when *Constitution*—the largest steamboat in the Texas trade, at 262 tons and 150 feet long—arrived. The river was too narrow for the vessel to turn around, and it was forced to back up until it reached a wide spot where it

25

could turn. The spot became known as Constitution Bend, and it is the site of the present Port of Houston's Turning Basin.

Despite snags, Houston developed into a popular transshipment point. By 1838, four steamboats regularly sailed between Houston and Galveston, and by 1840, at least one steamboat left Houston for Galveston every day. Boats carried passengers and agricultural goods to and from the Texas interior.

In 1841, the Houston City Council passed an ordinance establishing the Port of Houston, giving it authority over wharves, landings, slips, and roads on Buffalo Bayou within city limits. It could collect wharf fees to improve the port. The following year, the Republic of Texas's legislature authorized Houston to remove wrecked steamers from Buffalo Bayou and permitted a tonnage tax on ships entering the port. The city could now clear snags, remove obstructions, and turn upper Buffalo Bayou into a truly navigable channel.

The improbable port's importance grew during the 1850s when the railroad came to Texas. Houston, not Galveston, became the railroad center of Texas, as it was more centrally located and offered better overland access. Geography again helped; there was only one way to reach Galveston by rail, but Houston could be reached from many directions.

As important as the route soon became, the trip was still difficult. In addition to the natural limitations of Buffalo Bayou, Galveston Bay was shallow and crossed with reefs. Vessels that reached Houston were shallow draft, unsuitable for ocean travel. Their destination was almost always Galveston, where cargoes would be transferred to oceangoing vessels.

The two rivals continued as reluctant partners through the mid-19th century. The Civil War put a brake on growth, but afterward, business boomed. Demand for Texas cotton, cattle, and grain was growing, and Galveston had the best seaport in the state. Most of this cargo was funneled through Houston to reach Galveston.

Yet after the Civil War, Houston worried about the relationship. Both towns prospered, but should technology offer improved overland access to Galveston, Houston could find itself bypassed. In the 1870s, Houston's port lost its passenger traffic after railroad access to Galveston improved. Houston's cargo tonnage remained high, but Galveston was hiking rates for transshipped cargo to encourage direct overland shipping to and from that port. Houston's solution was to bypass Galveston, and the Houston Direct Shipping Company, created in 1869, developed a system of loading and unloading oceangoing vessels in Bolivar Roads at the mouth of Galveston Bay and transporting cargoes to and from Houston on barges. The ships skipped Galveston Harbor, avoiding harbor fees.

This was a partial solution. Houston wanted a deep-draft channel, and the Buffalo Bayou Ship Channel Company was chartered in 1869 with the goal of creating a nine-foot channel that would reach Main Street. In 1870, the federal government made Houston a port of entry, permitting international cargoes. A federal survey of a ship channel was authorized in 1870 and completed in January 1870. It recommended a channel at least 100 feet wide, and six feet deep.

The Panic of 1873 halted the work of the Buffalo Bayou Ship Channel Company. The Army Corps of Engineers dredged a channel across Galveston Bay, cutting through Red Fish Bar, which ran across the waist of the bay. The channel was 14.5 feet deep across the reef, but stopped short of Buffalo Bayou.

Enter New York–based shipping magnate Charles Morgan. His Morgan Line was one of the largest steamship companies in the Gulf of Mexico during the 1870s. In 1873, the Galveston Wharf Company withdrew free use of its facilities from the Morgan Line, and Morgan decided to make Houston his port. He bought up both the Houston Direct Shipping Company and the Buffalo Bayou Ship Channel Company. In 1874, he signed a contract to build a channel from Galveston Bay to Houston. It was to be 120 feet wide and 9 feet deep.

By 1876, Morgan had completed digging of a canal across Morgan's Point (named for an earlier and unrelated Morgan) and built a 250-foot turning basin where Sim's Bayou met Buffalo Bayou. In April 1876, the *Morgan*, an oceangoing side-wheeler that drew nine and a half feet, entered the new facility, making Houston a seaport—at least for smaller vessels.

VIEW ON THE BAYOU AT HOUSTON.

Buffalo Bayou at the site proposed for Houston was more suitable for small craft than for steamboats. Convincing investors that it was a port was an early example of what later would be labeled "Texas brag." (UHDL.)

Originally from New York, John Kirby Allen and his older brother Augustus began speculating in Texas in 1833. John died in Houston in 1838, two years after founding the town, and is now buried at Founders Memorial Cemetery. (HMM.)

Augustus Chapman Allen, along with his younger brother John Kirby, founded Houston. He named the city Houston based on a suggestion made by his wife. Augustus left Houston shortly after his brother's death, eventually returning to New York. (HMM.)

The original plat of Houston as developed by John and Augustus Allen shows a city on the south bank of Buffalo Bayou. The brothers advertised their new town as the premier location for a port in Texas, despite its unpromising location. (HMM.)

To demonstrate their claim that Houston could serve as a port, the Allens hired the steamship *Laura* to visit. It took the vessel two days to clear the snags between Harrisburg and Houston and compete the final five miles of the trip. This model is a modern interpretation of the *Laura*'s trip on the Buffalo Bayou. (AP-HMM.)

FOR THE CITY OF HOUSTON.
THE REGULAR
PACKET  STEAMER
LAURA,
T. W. GRAYSON, MASTER.

WILL leave Marion, on Tuesday, the 21st February, at 4 o'clock, P. M. for the above city, and all intermediate ports. For freight or passage apply on board; or to Aldridge and Davis, Marion, or to Thomas H. Borden, Columbia.

N. B.—The Laura, this trip, will touch at Anahuac.

Columbia, Feb. 20, 1837.   59-1

The Allen brothers announced the arrival of the steamboat *Laura* in Texas's newest seaport, Houston, in an advertisement posted in the *Telegraph and Texas Register*. (HMM.)

The first trips to the Port of Houston were adventures that occasionally took days and often saw passengers amusing themselves (as seen in this drawing) by hunting alligators then infesting the banks of Buffalo Bayou. (HMM.)

While Galveston is often cited as a competitor to Houston as a seaport, throughout the 1800s the two ports had a symbiotic relationship, with Galveston serving as the major destination for Houston cargoes. (LOC.)

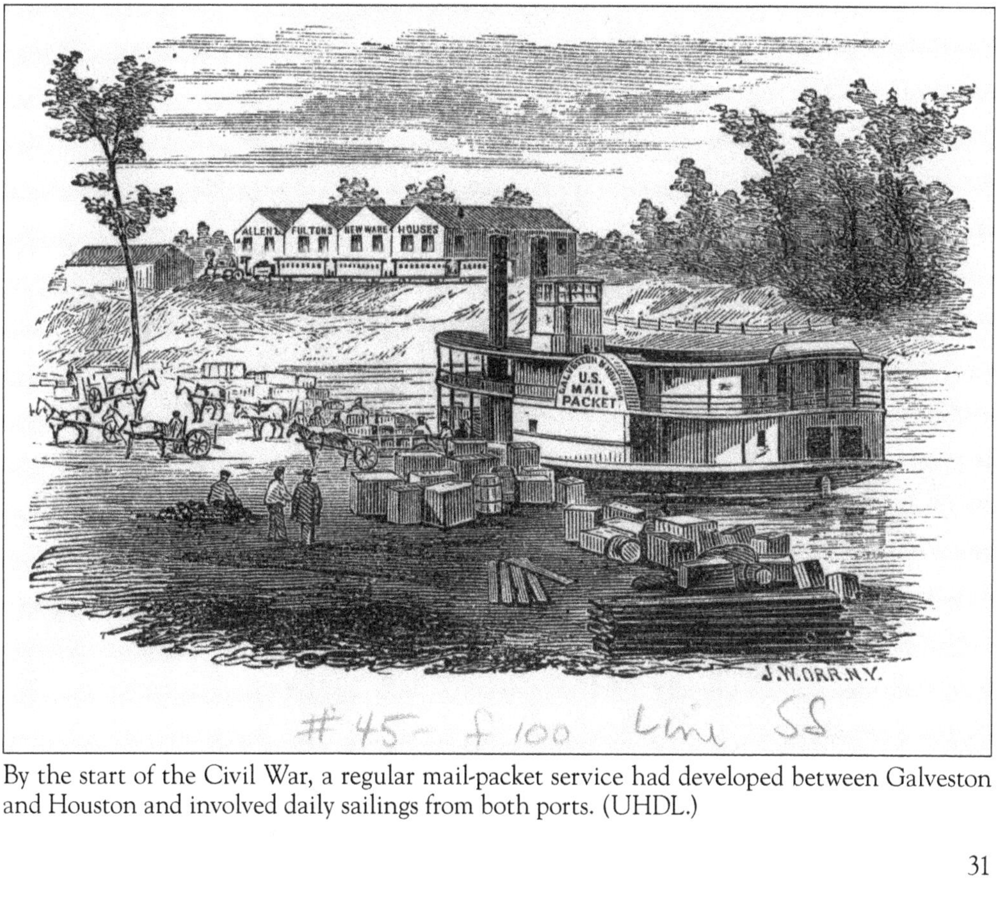

By the start of the Civil War, a regular mail-packet service had developed between Galveston and Houston and involved daily sailings from both ports. (UHDL.)

Until the railroads appeared, most of the cargo shipped from Houston either came by barge or was freighted overland in animal-drawn carts and wagons. Here, the steamboat *St. Clair* is at the foot of Main Street. (HMM.)

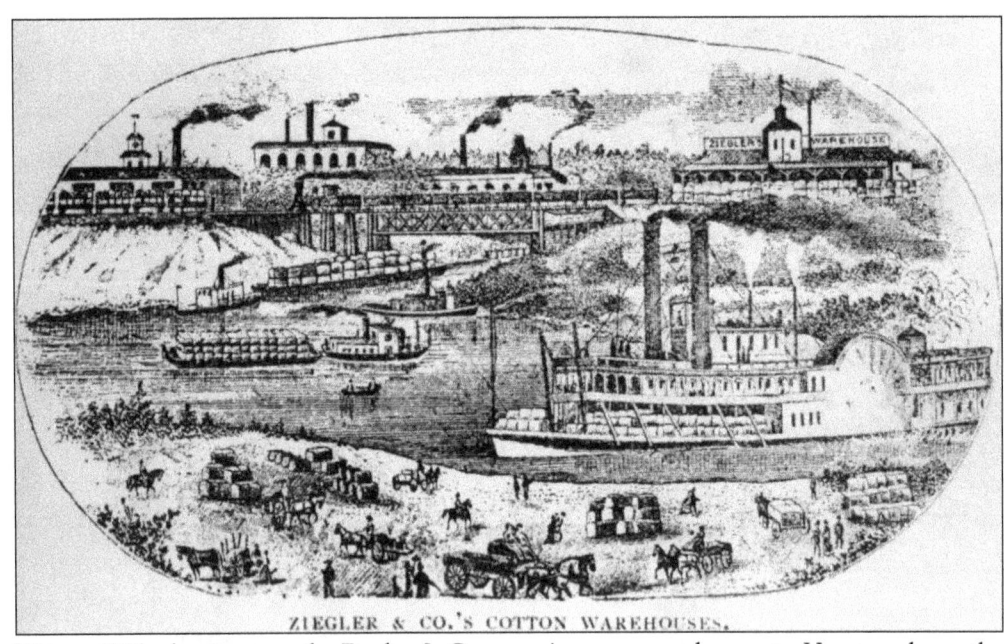

This c. 1866 advertisement for Ziegler & Company's cotton warehouses in Houston shows the nature of the port in the immediate aftermath of the Civil War. It was crowded with both barges and steamboats, and cotton brought in by railroad and wagon was a primary cargo. (UHDL.)

The side-wheeler *Diana* was built in 1870 and served Houston as a steamboat for nine years. In 1879, its engines were removed, and it was cut down into a barge. (HMM.)

The side-wheel steamer *Lizzie* is captured at the foot of Main Street during the 1870s. The ship was lost in 1880. (HMM.)

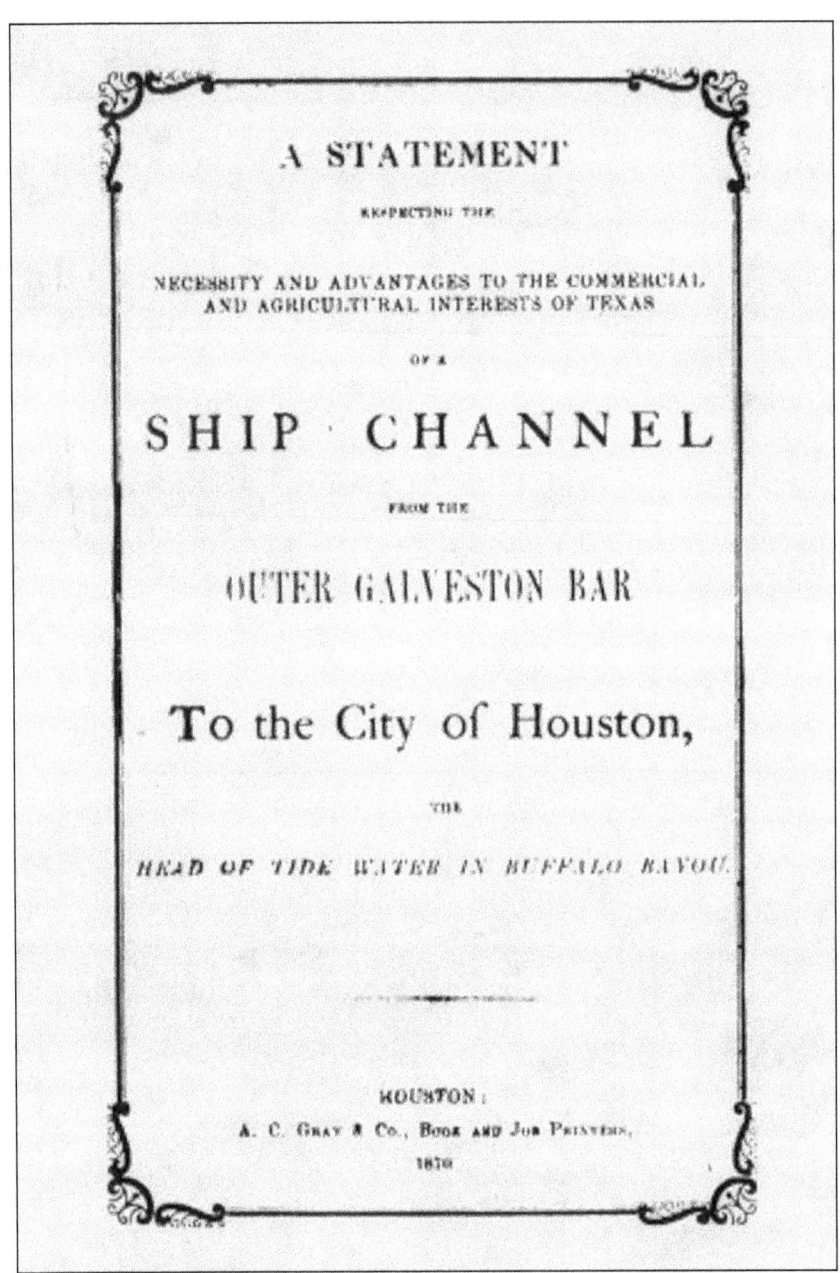

Even as early as 1870, Houston interests were publishing calls to deepen the Houston Ship Channel so that more oceangoing vessels could reach Houston. (UHDL.)

While not the Morgan for whom Morgan's Point was named, Charles Morgan was an important figure in Houston's development as a seaport. Owner of the Morgan Line, he dredged the first channel to Buffalo Bayou and helped convert Houston from a river port to a seaport. (HMM.)

By cutting through the land at Morgan's Point, Charles Morgan created a deepwater channel to Buffalo Bayou that avoided the shallow banks at Clopper's Point and shortened the trip to the Port of Houston. He also created a controversy by charging a fee for using the passage. (HMM.)

The SS *Morgan* was one of the seagoing steamships Charles Morgan owned and wished to send to Houston. It was one of the first vessels to use Morgan's canal to reach Houston. (HMM.)

In the years after the Civil War, the stretch of Buffalo Bayou near Allens' Landing had been abandoned by all but barges and shallow-draft ships. The port moved downstream closer to Harrisburg than the Allens' original location for Houston. (HMM.)

Railroads made Houston a seaport as much as the ship channel did. They allowed cargoes to be taken from Texas's interior directly to dockside. Houston's location made it easier to reach by rail than Galveston, giving Houston a competitive advantage. (HMM.)

Barges formed an important part of Houston's port traffic. The record for a load of cotton carried by barge was made in 1899 when the barge *Jackson* took 5,300 bales out of Houston. The cotton was transshipped to a seagoing steamer in Bolivar Roads. (HMM.)

Cotton had become such an important source of revenue for Houston and its port that the Houston Cotton Exchange & Board of Trade was founded in 1874 to facilitate its trade. This building, completed in 1884, served as its home until 1924. (LOC.)

Three

A Seaport Is Born

Despite the limited access to the ocean Houston gained in 1876, its claim to being a full-fledged seaport was more Texas brag than firm reality. Since a private corporation dug the Morgan's Point canal, its use was limited to Morgan Line ships and vessels that paid Morgan a toll. A chain was placed across the entrance to block passage and enforce Morgan's rules. After Morgan's death in 1878, his heirs offered to turn these improvements over to the federal government—for a fee. It was not until 1892 that these negotiations were completed, the chain removed, and the Houston Ship Channel established as a public thoroughfare.

Even before then, limited depth restricted the vessels that could use the channel to the smallest oceangoing ships. Ships with a 14-foot draft could use Galveston even in the 1870s, and Galveston was busy deepening its harbor. By 1897, the channel to Galveston had been deepened to 25 feet. This threatened Houston's lightering operations as deep-draft ships could now load at Galveston (rather than anchoring in Bolivar Roads and transferring cargoes from Houston barges).

Another threat to the Port of Houston was Morgan himself. He viewed Houston as a stopgap until the completion of a railroad from Houston to New Orleans. After the railroad was completed in 1880, Morgan's heirs began routing their traffic overland.

This combination eroded Houston's value as a port. By 1879, the Army Corps of Engineers had dredged a channel through Galveston Bay that met Morgan's canal. The drop-off in traffic led to suspension of appropriations to maintain and improve the channel between 1883 and 1888. The neglected channel began filling in, reducing its depth and usefulness.

Houston was unwilling to give up its dream of becoming a deepwater seaport. What geography had denied Houston—a deep channel—technology, in the form of dredges, could provide. As early as 1880, the Houston Cotton Exchange led efforts to improve navigation on Buffalo Bayou, prodding the federal government to straighten, deepen, and clear the waterway. This Buffalo Bayou project resulted in several federally funded studies of the issue between 1880 and 1896; however, little other than plans resulted.

In 1897, Houston congressman Thomas H. Ball became a member of the Rivers and Harbors Committee. His influence led to appropriations for a new survey of a water channel from the channel leading to Galveston's harbor to a new harbor at or near Houston. The channel was to be at least 25 feet deep and 100 feet wide, and the new Houston harbor would be 25 feet deep by 500 feet wide.

A US Army Corps of Engineers committee chaired by Col. Henry M. Robert met in Houston that July to examine the results of the survey and recommend further action. The plan, which specified dredging a 25-foot channel through Galveston Bay and then deepening Morgan's canal to the same depth, formed the basis of today's Houston Ship Channel. A width of 150 feet was recommended to compensate for deterioration. A second length, from the north end of the Morgan canal to Harrisburg, Texas, would follow Buffalo Bayou, improving the existing riverbed to a 100-foot-by-25-foot channel. A third stretch, from Harrisburg to Houston, would cut a new channel, removing one bend by a cutoff canal, and straightening and widening others. A turning basin was to be placed downstream of White Oak Bayou, roughly at Constitution Bend. It would be 500 feet by 25 feet.

The cost for the project was estimated at $4 million, and annual maintenance for the completed channel was estimated at $100,000. In 1898, the report was accepted by Congress and was folded into the Rivers and Harbors Act of 1899. A sum of $300,000 was appropriated in 1900 to begin construction.

The project's completion was uncertain. What Congress gave, Congress could take away. Some congressmen believed the undertaking to be an unnecessary boondoggle, given that a perfectly good port already existed at Galveston. Then, nature took a hand. In September 1900, a hurricane swept Galveston Island, inundating the city and destroying the harbor. Over 5,000 people died. Suddenly, a port 50 miles inland looked much safer than a port on a barrier island. Galveston rebuilt and put in a seawall, but much of the opposition to the idea of a ship channel to Houston had faded.

The easy parts of the project were the ones finished first. By 1903, work began on the channel across Galveston Bay. It was to be 150 feet wide but dredged only to a depth of 18.5 feet. In 1904, the uppermost terminus of the channel was set. Instead of continuing to the foot of Main Street, the Turning Basin was placed at what became the head of Long Reach—two miles below Main Street and two miles above Harrisburg. In addition, to straighten the route, three cut-offs were approved. One cut across the loop of Irish Bend, a second straightened Clinton Bend, and the third bypassed Harrisburg. Work began on these in 1905 and 1906.

Progress was too slow to satisfy Houston interests. The Houston Ship Channel was still unfinished by 1908, despite having been authorized a decade earlier. Additionally, the authorized depth—18.5 feet—was viewed as inadequate. A 25-foot depth was needed. Construction of the Panama Canal, having started in 1901, was advanced by 1908, and Houstonians wanted a harbor that could accommodate ships that used the canal.

Cutting a channel through the mud and dirt of Buffalo Bayou and Galveston Bay was easy. The problem was that the Washington of 1900 was tight-fisted, allocating and releasing money at a trickle. Houstonians, deciding things would move faster with a little more cash, offered Washington a deal. Houston would provide half the money to finish the channel—a 25-foot-deep channel—if Washington would match it.

Local contributions toward a federal navigation project had never previously occurred. After receiving assurance that the port would be publicly owned, Congress bought in, adding the Houston Ship Channel to the Rivers and Harbors Act of 1910. It authorized $2.5 million for the project, half to be provided by a local navigation district.

The Texas Legislature passed legislation in 1909 authorizing the creation of a navigation district with the ability to issue bonds and collect taxes. Local voters created the Harris County Ship Channel Navigation District in 1911 and passed a $1,250,000 bond issue. The infusion of money worked. Work began on the deeper channel in 1912, and over the next two years, 23 million cubic yards of spoil was dredged.

The 25-foot-deep Houston Ship Channel was officially completed on September 7, 1914. Pres. Woodrow Wilson presided at the opening ceremony on November 10. At least two ships had arrived before then: the *William C. May*, a schooner with a 16.5-foot draft, had docked September 26, 1914, and the *Dorothy*, a 290-foot-long Bull Line steamer that drew 19 feet, had arrived October 12. Houston had a seaport.

This detail from a bird's-eye-view map shows the Houston Ship Channel and the Port of Houston in 1891. Lacking a deepwater channel across Galveston Bay, the port was only navigable to the small steamers and barges shown on the map. (LOC.)

As the 20th century neared, cotton was king at the port. In 1899, a total of 2,543,059 bales shipped through Houston, and local newspapers brag about the accomplishment in this political cartoon. (HMM.)

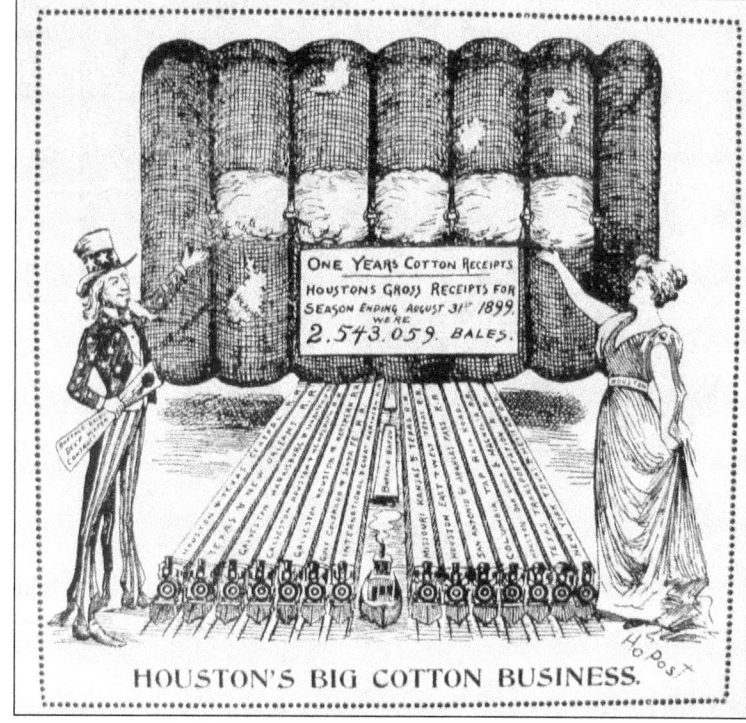

A three-masted schooner sits moored in the Houston Ship Channel in the 1890s. Sailing ships like this still carried coastal cargoes at that time but required the assistance of tugs to negotiate the narrow channel. (HMM.)

Henry Martyn Robert, author of *Robert's Rules of Order*, believed Galveston should be the major port on the Gulf Coast. While in the Army Corps of Engineers, he participated in the design of the Galveston Seawall. Yet he also led the board overseeing the survey of the Houston Ship Channel and produced testimony critical to the channel's approval in 1901 Congressional hearings. (HMM.)

The 1900 hurricane that swept over Galveston destroyed the island city and its port but largely spared Houston. The event strengthened calls to deepen the ship channel and make Houston accessible to large oceangoing ships. (LOC.)

This is a side view of the snag boat *Waco*. Like most river-clearing vessels of that era, the *Waco* was shallow-draft and flat-bottomed and used a stern-mounted paddle wheel rather than employing propellers. (HMM.)

Here, the dredge *Waco* moored on the bank of a Texas river. *Waco* was one of the boats used by the Galveston District of the Corps of Engineers to remove snags, deepen channels, and make estuaries, like Buffalo Bayou, navigable. Both images of *Waco* were taken at the same time and place. (HMM.)

Cotton remained an important cargo for the Port of Houston into the 20th century, but by the time of this 1904 photograph, most arrived at the port by rail. (LOC.)

The dredge *Washington* deepens the Turning Basin in 1910. The Turning Basin would become the heart of the port during the 20th century. (HMM.)

Even after the big ships moved downstream from the foot of Main Street, barges and tugs still moored there. This photograph was taken before construction of the Main Street Viaduct, which closed off part of this area. (HMM.)

Construction of the Panama Canal, shown here, was one factor that drove efforts to deepen the Houston Ship Channel. The canal was expected to cause an increase in Gulf of Mexico traffic, which Houston wanted a part of. That required a channel that the ships that traversed the Panama Canal could also use. (LOC.)

The Main Street Viaduct, built in 1911, limited access to the portions of Buffalo Bayou west of the bridge. It effectively shut part of what had been the old port of Houston. (UHDL.)

The *San Jacinto* was one of the dredges built for the federal government to construct the original Houston Ship Channel. Larger than earlier dredges, it was delivered in 1911. (HMM.)

Once the upper reaches of Buffalo Bayou became impractical for embarking commercial cargoes, the location became the place where excursion boats, yachts, and personal craft were moored. (HMM.)

By 1912, Houston had grown into a major city, its expansion fueled by its port and ship channel, even before the largest ships could reach it. (LOC.)

Another sign that Houston was transforming into a world-class seaport was the construction of a new and modern customhouse, completed in 1912. (LOC.)

OFFICE OF
ATTORNEY GENERAL
OF
STATE OF TEXAS. No. 695.

This is to certify, That the **Harris County** — County, Texas, **Houston Ship Channel Navigation District of Harris** bonds, issued by virtue of an **Order** passed by the **Commissioners Court** of said **County** on the **12th** day of **May, 1911**, for the purpose of **dredging and deepening what is known as Houston Ship Channel to a depth of twenty-five feet, to be made navigable by seagoing vessels** dated **June 1st, 1911**, numbered consecutively from **1** to **1248** inclusive, for the sum of **$1,000.** and Nos. **1249 to 1252 both inclusive for Five Hundred** Dollars each, aggregating the sum of **One Million Two Hundred and Fifty Thousand** Dollars, payable at **County Treasury, Houston, Texas; National Bank of the Republic, Chicago, Illinois at option of holder, 40 years** payable one-fourth every ten years with interest at the rate of **4-1/2** per cent per annum, payable **semi-annually June & Dec. 1st** have been submitted to me for examination in accordance with the requirements of Article 918d, Revised Statutes of Texas, 1895, and I have carefully examined said bonds in connection with the facts and the Constitution and laws on the subject of the execution of said bonds, and I find upon the evidence submitted to me and as the result of a careful examination of the matter the following facts:

1. Said **Houston Ship Channel Navigation District** of **Harris County** was at the time of the passage of the **Order** above referred to legally **Established**.
2. The taxable values of said **District** according to the assessment last approved before the issuance of said bonds amounted to **$121,137,985.00**
3. The debt of said **District** for the purposes for which said bonds were issued was increased by said issue to the sum of **$1,250,000.00** the total indebtedness of said **District** was hereby increased in the sum of

One Million Two Hundred and Fifty Thousand ($1,250,000.00) Dollars

4. The **Order** authorizing the issuance of said bonds is in proper form and was legally passed.
5. A tax of **eight and one-third** cents on each one hundred dollars valuation of taxable property in said **District** was legally levied to pay interest on said bonds and to create a sinking fund to provide for their liquidation at maturity; said tax is sufficient for the purposes named.
6. Said bonds are proper in form and in accordance with the **Order** authorizing their issuance and all the requirements of the law under which they were issued have been complied with.

It is my judgment and I so find that said bonds were issued in conformity with the Constitution and laws of the State of Texas and that they are valid and binding obligations upon said **Houston Ship Channel Navigation District** of **Harris County**, Texas.

In Testimony of all which this certificate is made under my hand and the seal of my office at Austin, Texas, this the **4th** day of **January** A.D. **1912**.

Attorney General of Texas

This certificate is for one of the bonds issued by Harris County in 1912 to finance the dredging of the ship channel to a depth of 25 feet. The bond paid four and a half percent interest semiannually. (UHDL.)

The Houston Ship Channel in 1913 was far from the impressive industrial giant it would become later that century. One year before the completion of dredging, it was often the preserve of small craft only. (POHA.)

The opening ceremony for the port was held on September 7, 1914. It marked the completion of the dredging of the deepwater channel and opened the port to oceangoing ships—a capability that would be exploited throughout World War I, which began around the same time that the port opened. (POHA.)

Four

THE OPENING YEARS

Houston now had a channel by which oceangoing ships could reach it, though its wharves, docks, and warehouses were scaled for a smaller port. Additionally, ship captains were reluctant to try the unfamiliar channel on their own. Only a handful of ships arrived in the first six months after the port opened, the total further reduced by the outbreak of World War I, which discouraged shipping. To lure regular shipping service to the port, local businessmen decided to sweeten the pot with a $100,000 bond to cover any potential losses incurred serving Houston.

The Southern Shipping Company, which received the guarantee, refused the offered bond and agreed to make Houston a scheduled stop anyway. The first arrival, SS *Satilla*, left New York for Houston in August 1915.

The ship arrived in the wake of the 1915 Hurricane. Galveston's newly completed seawall protected that city from inundation, but overland routes to the island were once again cut off. The storm flooded Morgan's Point and washed away some of the Houston Ship Channel's navigation markers. Yet the channel was undamaged, and the *Satilla* arrived safely on August 23, with 1,925 tons of cargo aboard. It was first of many arrivals by Southern Steamship Company, and by 1918 the line was the largest general-freight shipper at the Port of Houston.

Houston was off to a slow start, regardless. In 1919, the port registered only 157 arrivals and 1,287,972 tons of cargo. In 1920, there were 165 arrivals and 1,219,204 tons of cargo. Galveston, by contrast, recorded 714 arrivals and 2,348,477 tons of cargo between July 1, 1919, and June 30, 1920.

That was about to change. Houston voters went to the poll in late 1914 to authorize a $3 million bond issue to pay for the warehouses, wharves, and other terminal facilities the port lacked. By 1920, the first of these facilities had been completed—three docks, including a 1,303-foot concrete dock, three concrete warehouses, cotton-storage sheds, and a railroad to link these to Houston main lines. All were located along the Turning Basin, giving Long Reach an appearance it retains today. The channel to the foot of Main Street was also improved, deepened to 8 feet and widened to 40 feet, to improve barge access to the turning basin.

The boom in petroleum consumption following World War I created skyrocketing demand for oil-based products. Petroleum emerged as a major factor along the Houston Ship Channel, which offered everything a petroleum refinery needed: deepwater access, plenty of fresh water, abundant land (most of the channel between the Turning Basin and Morgan's Point was undeveloped), and most importantly, sufficient elevation. It was one of the few areas near the Texas oil fields high enough to minimize flooding from tropical storms or hurricanes. By 1918, six major oil companies had built or were building large refineries along the channel. Humble Oil's Goose Creek facility, completed in 1919, eventually became the largest refinery in the United States.

As the decade ended, most petroleum was transported on the ship channel on barges. Tankers grew faster than other ships of that era, and tankers drawing 27 to 30 feet had become common by 1920. Even without the large tankers, petroleum was already the port's biggest import, accounting for 72 percent of incoming tonnage. As a result, five years after completing the 25-foot channel, Houston clamored to deepen the ship channel. In 1919, to accommodate the large tankers, Army engineers approved dredging the channel to a 30-foot depth. Congress appropriated funds for two years later, and the project was completed by 1925.

Negotiating the Houston Ship Channel was also addressed in the years between 1914 and 1920. Individuals began receiving appointments as branch pilots—certified to provide navigation services in the channel—as early as 1916. These pilots, possessing and having demonstrated a knowledge of the channel, assumed responsibility for taking a ship from Bolivar Roads to a berth along the channel or from the Port of Houston to Bolivar Roads. By 1919, over a dozen pilots were certified, sufficient to conn the few hundred ships that visited Houston annually. In 1921, a Houston Pilots Association formed, and in 1923 Texas passed an act creating a commission to certify and regulate pilots. Professional pilots made Houston much more attractive.

The final piece to the puzzle of how to turn Houston into a major seaport also fell into place in 1919, when Benjamin C. Allin was hired as the first director of the Port of Houston. Educated at the University of Chicago, Allin was an engineer and had worked for two railroads and a steel company prior to World War I. During the war, he commanded a US Army combat-engineer company in France. Following his discharge after the war, he came to Houston seeking opportunities in the oil business. Instead, he was asked to lead development of the new port. Allin served as director until 1930 as it grew from a stuttering start into the nation's third-largest port.

Things just came together for the port in the 1920s. The deepening of the channel accelerated the growth of the petroleum industry and also facilitated Houston's role as a cotton port. More cotton could be loaded into larger ships at Houston's wharves, reducing Houston's dependence on transshipping on barges to Bolivar Roads or the Port of Galveston. Ship arrivals at the port doubled between 1919 and 1921, doubled again by 1923, doubled again in 1926, and topped 2,100 in 1930. Houston passed Galveston during that decade, a lead it never relinquished.

Port facilities also expanded during the period. A new terminal was opened at Manchester, where Sims Bayou meets Buffalo Bayou, from land donated in 1917. It was the first port terminal built outside what were then the city limits of Houston, and it signaled that Houston's port would not be limited to the Turning Basin but would spread along the Houston Ship Channel. A grain elevator was completed in 1926, adding grain to the mix of cargoes shipped from Houston. The elevator had an initial capacity of three million bushels but was expanded to 3,500,000 in the early 1930s.

By 1927, eight refineries lined the Houston Ship Channel, capable of processing 125,000 barrels of crude oil daily. Three petroleum tankers passed through the channel every day, tying up at one of 19 berths privately owned by the various oil companies on the channel.

Other needed port infrastructure was added in the 1920s, although some things were added later than they should have been. A 1924 fire aboard a ship loading cotton underscored a need for firefighting facilities with more flexibility than fire trucks could provide. Funds were authorized for the port's first fireboat in 1925. The vessel, *Port Houston*, was delivered in 1926, and helped fight six refinery fires in its first year of service. It served until 1950.

As the 1920s ended, the Port of Houston shipped nearly two million bales of cotton, over eleven million tons of petroleum, and nearly five million bushels of grain. The Port of Houston had arrived—but so had the Great Depression.

The Panama Canal also had its opening in 1914. By improving access to Pacific ports from the Gulf of Mexico, it increased Houston's importance as a seaport. (LOC.)

Satilla's arrival at the Port of Houston in August 1915 marked the beginning of scheduled steamship service to Houston. Its arrival was a cause for celebration and drew large crowds. (UHDL.)

While Galveston's new seawall kept the 1915 hurricane from inundating the community, its railroad causeway (as shown in this picture) was washed away, again leaving the Port of Galveston isolated. (UHDL.)

Tug *E.M. Hartrick* was launched in 1916. Named for one of the men who oversaw construction of the Houston Ship Channel, it served in Galveston and the Houston Ship Channel until 1939. It was typical of the tugboats used in the channel during its early years. (HMM.)

While cotton remained an important export for Houston in the first decade after the port opened, petroleum finds in Texas created another commodity important to both Houston and its port. The first refinery on the Houston Ship Channel opened in 1919. (LOC.)

The steamship *San Jacinto* is pictured in the Houston Ship Channel shortly after its opening. While Houston would not surpass Galveston's tonnage for several years, it was on its way to becoming the biggest port in Texas. (HMM.)

Benjamin C. Allin was the Port of Houston's first director. His tenure ran from 1919 through 1930. (HMM.)

This is the Houston Ship Channel and Turning Basin in the 1920s, according to a promotional brochure put together by Port of Houston boosters. As depicted here, a spacious port awaits shippers. (UHDL.)

This was the reality of the Houston Ship Channel and Turning Basin in the 1920s as viewed from an aerial photograph. Note the limited number of berths and warehouses compared to later photographs (UHDL.)

HOUSTON SHIP CHANNEL FACTS

A Land-Locked Inland Harbor — Safe and Secure Harborage at All Times

Compare Your Present Freight Rates with the Rates Available Through this New Port and See the Enormous Saving to Your Business

Vol. 1   December, 1915   No. 1

COPYRIGHT, 1915, BY JULIA CAMERON MONTGOMERY

To promote the new port, boosters published *Houston Ship Channel Facts*, a brochure touting the new port's advantages and competitive freight rates. (UHDL.)

Passengers board an excursion steamer on the Buffalo Bayou in 1920. A day on the river was a popular diversion in Houston in an age before air-conditioning. (HMM.)

The excursion steamer *Nicholaus* carries a crowd of passengers touring Buffalo Bayou in the 1920s. Freight traffic was not yet dominating the waterway. (HMM.)

Navigating the Houston Ship Channel required intimate knowledge of 50 miles of waterways. Pilot boats, such as *Houston Pilot Boat No. 1*, carried such pilots to the vessels seeking access to the port. (AP-HMM.)

The pilot leaves the pilot boat for the ship to be conned into the Port of Houston. He will board the ship using a Jacob's ladder, and ship channel pilots still board vessels in Bolivar Roads in this way. (HMM.)

The ships in 1922 were smaller than those seen at the Houston docks at the end of the break-bulk era, and more manual labor was used, but ships were loaded in the same way that they had been for generations. (HMM.)

A tug shepherds a tanker through the Houston Ship Channel in the 1920s. The vessel is somewhere between the San Jacinto Battlefield and Galena Park, an area that was then largely undeveloped. (HMM.)

City of Fort Worth moored at the Port of Houston after World War I. The ship belonged to Southern Steamship Company, which was the first shipper to establish service to Houston and the corporate descendant of the shipping company founded by Charles Morgan (HMM.)

Bags of flour are loaded aboard a ship at the Port of Houston. The use of machinery is minimal, limited to the crane running the hoist. Next, longshoremen will position the individual bags into the hold. (UHDL.)

The fireboat *Port Houston* was built in 1925 and entered service at the port the following year. Its construction was authorized following a 1924 fire in the hold of a cotton ship at the port. (HMM.)

Mechanization in the 1920s often meant the use of a steam crane for loading cargo. (UHDL.)

A dedication ceremony was held for the Public Grain Elevator (later Public Grain Elevator No. 1) when it opened in 1926. Grain was always important to Houston. The first public elevator in Houston, which this replaced, was built in 1875. This grain elevator had a capacity of 6.3 million bushels. (HMM.)

The sailing frigate USS *Constitution* arrived in the Houston Ship Channel in 1932. Over 100,000 visitors boarded the ship during its four-and-a-half-day visit to Houston following the frigate's refit in the 1920s. (HMM.)

Five

DEPRESSION AND WAR

Over a two-day period culminating on October 29, 1929, the Dow Jones Industrial Average dropped 25 percent. The day, known as Black Tuesday, marked the start of 12 years of economic downturn known as the Great Depression.

The United States was not alone in economic misery. The London Stock Exchange had crashed a month earlier on September 20. Economies collapsed throughout Europe. This, in turn, reduced the demand for goods from supplier nations in South America and European colonies in Asia and Africa. The world was soon mired in depression.

The Smoot-Hawley Act passed in 1930, dramatically increasing import tariffs. Other nations increased their tariffs in retaliation, further reducing maritime trade. Protectionism proved an international version of the prisoner's dilemma; if one nation had high tariffs, it won big, while the others lost big. When everyone had high tariffs, everyone lost.

The Port of Houston depended on trade. Yet the Depression years resulted in lost growth and forgone opportunity rather than just lost jobs and lost cargoes. Ship arrivals dipped in 1931, and cargo tonnage shrank in 1931 and 1932. By 1933, though, both ship arrivals and cargo tonnage exceeded that of 1930. For the rest of the decade, both grew—albeit more slowly than they had during the 1920s. In 1939, ship arrivals and tonnage exceeded the 1930 totals by 50 percent.

Some parts of the port got hammered, however. Worldwide demand for grain plunged due to the Smoot-Hawley Tariff and global insolvency. Grain exports, which exceeded five million bushels in 1930, collapsed two years later. Less than three million bushels were exported in 1932. In 1933, the grain elevator shut down. For the next five years, the elevator employed only a small crew for maintenance, and it only resumed exporting grain in 1938.

Additionally, the values of the cargo shipped also dropped, demand for luxury goods fell, and commodity prices went down. Increased tonnage made up part of the lost value, but not until 1939—which saw 60 percent more tonnage than 1930—did the value of the cargoes shipped exceed that of 1930.

Less labor was required to unload the ships that did arrive, especially from the last half of 1930 through 1932, when fewer ships arrived. Pay scales dropped with the demand for labor, and labor unrest resulted, with virtually annual strikes. A particularly ugly longshoremen's strike in 1935 lasted 10 weeks. Steamship lines imported strikebreakers from East Texas, and to counter the resulting violence, the port created a force to police the waterfront. In the end, as with a seamen's strike the following year, labor and management fought to stalemate. Neither side won; perhaps both lost.

Technology again worked to Houston's benefit during the Depression. Long-haul trucking arrived in the 1930s. Trucks could reach more places and were more flexible than railroads, allowing truckers to successfully compete. Setting up a trucking company required little capital, and the trucking industry was then unregulated, allowing men displaced by the Depression to set themselves up as independent truckers.

To these men, distance traveled was money burned. Stopping at Houston instead of Galveston cut 50 miles from the trip when arriving from the north or west, and it was preferable to save money with the nearer stop. Cargo that might have been shipped out of Galveston had it traveled by rail ended up at the Port of Houston instead.

Galveston was not the only port cannibalized by Houston with the rise of trucking. Cotton from Arkansas and Oklahoma that had previously flowed to New Orleans was instead trucked to Houston. To recapture traffic, New Orleans revived Mississippi River basin barge traffic, teaming with railroads to provide rail-barge service.

While the Depression slowed expansion, it did not eliminate it. The Houston Ship Channel was deepened to 34 feet in the 1930 and was widened to 400 feet through Galveston Bay and 300 feet through Morgan's Point. The drought in industrial construction along the ship channel broke in 1936, when Champion Paper broke ground for a paper mill in Pasadena, Texas, making wood pulp another cargo for the port. It was the first plant constructed since 1929.

Although 1938 saw a downturn in the national economy, Houston and its port turned the corner in 1937. Grain exports resumed in 1936. Traffic was increasing, with scrap iron joining cotton and petroleum as major cargoes for the port. But before the port could achieve its full potential, it experienced another detour: World War II.

The war did what the Depression could not do—significantly reduce the Port of Houston's traffic. The port peaked in 1939, the year World War II began, with over 3,000 arrivals and cargo tonnage in excess of 28 million tons. Traffic slid slightly in 1940, dropped to two-thirds of the 1939 arrivals in 1941, then dropped below 1,000 ships per year over the next three years. The US Merchant Marine went to war.

When the United States entered the war in 1941, all scheduled commercial sailings were suspended. European-bound convoys departed from Atlantic ports, Pacific-bound convoys from Pacific ports, and Gulf Coast departures plummeted. Shipments that were made from Houston were war-related.

While the port's commercial traffic suffered, the Houston Ship Channel was busier than ever. Its refineries produced high-octane aviation gasoline and toluene (an ingredient for explosives). Two plants for the manufacture of synthetic rubber (made from petroleum by-products) were completed along the channel in 1943.

The location of the Houston Ship Channel, 50 miles from the coast, sheltered it from submarines, and the available deep water made it an ideal spot for war-related shipbuilding. Shipyards sprouted like mushrooms.

To build Liberty ships—war emergency-cargo ships—Todd Shipbuilding's Texas subsidiary, Houston Shipbuilding Company, constructed a shipyard at largely undeveloped Irish Bend Island (an island since the Houston Ship Channel cut across it in 1904) in 1941. Slow and powered by reciprocating steam engines, Liberty Ships were cheap and quickly built. By war's end, the new yard had delivered 66 Liberty Ships. Brown & Root built a yard where Green's Bayou met the Houston Ship Channel, where it built subchasers and destroyer escorts. Its most famous product, destroyer escort *Samuel B. Roberts*, fought Japan's main battle fleet at the Battle of Leyte Gulf.

The Houston Ship Channel was further deepened, straightened, and widened during the war. Additional defense plants were built during that period, including the massive San Jacinto Ordnance Depot. Many later privatized, providing potential peacetime customers for the port once the war ended in 1945. The Port of Houston was about to come into its own.

The Turning Basin and Long Reach docks had grown by the 1930s, though the effects of the Great Depression can be seen. While the harbor is crowded, it is not nearly at its full capacity. (POHA.)

Longshoremen load rice into a Garcia Lines freighter during the 1930s. While pallets were used to move the rice to the ship, longshoremen would then place individual bags into position in the hold. (HMM.)

Cotton is being transferred from railroad boxcars to a freighter in the Port of Houston. Even during the Great Depression, cotton remained an important cargo for the Houston Ship Channel. (HMM.)

Longshoremen load cotton into a freighter during the 1930s. Even into the fourth decade of the 20th century, cotton was a labor-intensive cargo, with bales handled individually. (HMM.)

Trucks, especially used trucks run by single-owner operators, fueled growth at the Port of Houston during the Depression. Eliminating the extra 50 miles to Galveston meant the difference between a loss and profit to these men. (UHDL.)

A truck crane moves a workboat at the Port of Houston. The boat is probably used for fishing or shrimping. (UHDL.)

Timber and wood pulp from East Texas was another cargo shipped to the Port of Houston once the Champion paper mill opened in 1936. (LOC.)

A large tugboat moves at full speed down the Houston Ship Channel in 1937. As the size of the freighters that used the Port of Houston grew, so too did the size and power of the tugboats there. (NARA.)

A Du Pont chemical plant on the Houston Ship Channel silhouettes on the horizon as a boy fishes on the opposite bank. By 1937, chemical and petroleum processing was a major industry along Buffalo Bayou. (NARA.)

A freighter outbound from the Port of Houston is pictured here in 1939. Partly loaded with cotton, it will load most of its cargo at Galveston or Bolivar Roads. (LOC.)

Texaco had an oil-storage facility along the Houston Ship Channel in 1939. The building facing the water is the receiving facility. Storage tanks can be seen in the background. (LOC.)

This plant for crushing oyster shells was typical of the industries that lined banks of the Houston Ship Channel. The crushed shells were used for cement, roads, and fertilizer. The channel provided access for receiving shells and shipping product to industrial users. (LOC.)

An industrial plant is pictured on the banks of the Houston Ship Channel in 1939. When the United States entered World War II two years later, facilities like these would contribute to America becoming the "Arsenal of Democracy." (LOC.)

Even as late as 1939, major sections of the Houston Ship Channel along Buffalo Bayou were undeveloped, resembling its appearance from a century earlier, when Houston was founded. (LOC.)

M10 tank destroyers are loaded aboard a Liberty Ship at the Long Reach docks in the Port of Houston. This load was probably headed for Europe. The public grain elevator can be seen in the background. (HMM.)

This DUWK amphibious truck is being loaded into a cargo ship at the Port of Houston late in World War II. DUWKs were used extensively in both Pacific and European theaters. (UHDL.)

Longshoremen push a DUWK amphibious truck into position in the hold of a cargo ship at the Port of Houston. Military cargoes and war materials dominated the port in World War II. (UHDL.)

Ship construction boomed during World War II, with much of it focused on small merchant ships and naval escort vessels built in a modular fashion to speed the process. (UHDL.)

The battleship USS *Texas* is photographed here during World War II. Built in 1914, it saw combat in two world wars. In 1946, the *Texas* was permanently moored at the San Jacinto Battlefield Park along the Houston Ship Channel. (HMM.)

This view shows the Turning Basin and Long Reach docks as they appeared after World War II, in 1946. Business is booming. Every berth at the Long Reach docks is filled, and across Buffalo Bayou, at the bulk-grain terminal, a ship is taking cargo while a second awaits its turn. (UHDL.)

Six

THE BRAWNY YEARS

The end of World War II marked a new era at the Port of Houston. The port that visionaries imagined when the Houston Ship Channel was planned had become reality. Facilities developed following World War I, the improvements and industries added during the 1920s, and the big industrial build-up along the channel in World War II created a mature port with natural customers.

Initially, there were fears that the traffic that had disappeared during World War II would never return. Local thinking believed that shippers, having grown accustomed to using Atlantic and Pacific ports, would ignore the Gulf Coast in the postwar world.

Those fears proved unfounded. With the arrival of peace and an end to convoying, ships flooded back to the Port of Houston. Almost as many ships arrived at Houston in the final four months of 1945 following the war's end on September 2, 1945, as had entered in the eight months of war preceding peace. Ship arrivals for 1945 were almost double those of 1944, and cargo tonnage increased from 17 million to 24 million. The year 1946 was even better; ship arrivals totaled 2,057, and cargo tonnage topped 31 million tons, breaking the annual tonnage record set in 1939.

One of the nation's biggest shipping companies, family-owned Lykes Line, had Texas connections, including a major presence in Houston and Galveston. Postwar rebuilding in Europe and Asia required raw materials. The Liberty Ships, Victory Ships, and other war-construction cargo vessels were surplus to military needs, and the US government disposed of them, selling them to shipping lines at bargain prices. Grain, cotton, and petroleum products flowed out of the port.

Annual total arrivals would not exceed the 1939 record until 1950, when 3,271 ships visited Houston. Because ships were bigger, annual cargo tonnage was well above that of 1946 totals for the entire period. Cargo tonnage continued growing throughout the 1950s and exceeded 60 million tons in 1959, more than double what it had been prior to World War II.

Traffic was up, although more variable, bouncing between 3,400 and 4,500 ships annually. An average of 10 ships a day entered the Houston Ship Channel in the 1950s.

The flood of traffic in the immediate postwar years strained the port's capacity. Port facilities needed to be refurbished. Maintenance had been deferred during the war years. Postwar projects to expand started before the war's end when Houston voters approved the issuing of bonds in December 1944. The port authority purchased all port facilities owned by the City of Houston in 1945. After that, local responsibility for running the port was the assumed by Port of Houston Authority, consolidating public operations at the port.

Improvements did not really begin until 1947. The postwar housing and construction boom soaked up available resources, and inflation shrank the value of moneys allocated for port improvements. The first improvement was made on the federal level. Funds were allocated in 1945 to deepen the channel to 36 feet over its entire length, and the channel was again widened in the postwar 1940s.

Locally funded improvements included construction of two highway tunnels under the Houston Ship Channel. Population around the channel had grown explosively during the war years, but there were then no bridges across Buffalo Bayou east of the Main Street Viaduct in downtown Houston. The only way for motor vehicles to cross the channel downstream of it was by ferry. The Washburn Tunnel, completed in 1950, linked Pasadena with Galena Park. The Baytown Tunnel, finished in 1953, connected La Port with Baytown. Both were only two lanes, but they simplified the chore of motoring across the channel.

Another postwar improvement was replacement of *Port Houston*, the port's fireboat. In 1947, two ships filled with fertilizer in Texas City's port burned and then exploded, focusing attention on port fire safety. *Port Houston* was replaced with a then state-of-the-art fireboat, *Captain Crotty*, in 1950.

Once the immediate postwar improvements were completed, the early 1950s saw enhancements around the Houston Ship Channel that came from the private sector and the addition of industrial facilities, rather than expansion of the port facilities. A major refinery replaced the Liberty Ship factory at Irish Bend Island, and other industrial facilities sprung up, spurring automobile traffic in the new tunnels.

There were several reasons for the stall in port expansion: Shipping demand fell off once the surge of postwar demand for American reconstruction goods declined. The St. Lawrence Seaway opened in 1954, providing ocean access to the Midwest. Cargoes that would have been sent to Houston were diverted to Great Lakes ports like Chicago, instead. New Orleans overhauled its port facilities, determined to regain dominance over Houston.

The Port of Houston remained busy, but during the first half of the 1950s, additional growth that would have spurred new facilities did not occur. Indeed, Houston, which had been the nation's second-busiest port (behind New York City) from 1948 through 1954, slipped to third place in 1955 when Philadelphia inched ahead of it.

Cargo handling had remained static for well over 40 years. Goods arrived at Houston in railcar-, wagon-, and later truckloads. Individual bags, bales, barrels, or crates were loaded aboard a ship by brawny men who unloaded the railcars, wagons, and trucks, and then muscled the freight into position in the hold.

By the 1950s, forklifts replaced handcarts, and machinery hoisted cargoes to and from the ships. A new innovation that had appeared in the war years was the practice of loading cargo onto pallets instead of placing individual bags and crates into cargo nets or rolling barrels and bales aboard on gangways, as had been the custom in the 1920s and 1930s.

To get this packaged cargo into and off a ship required its bulk to be broken down into man-sized units. It was called break-bulk cargo. Oil and other liquids were pumped into tankers, and bulk cargoes like grain could be poured into ships.

Despite mechanization, handling cargo remained labor-intensive in the 1950s. Even in a port like Houston, ships carrying break-bulk cargo took days, sometimes a week, to unload and load. Gangs of longshoremen were required. Shipping was expensive.

By 1956, Houstonians worried about the future of their port. It was a focus of pride. An observation platform was erected at the port so tourists could entertain themselves by watching harbor activity. Yet it seemed to be falling behind new ports that had been developed along the Texas coast, old rivals like New Orleans, and even an upstart port like Chicago. A major expansion of port facilities was planned and funded in 1957, with more wharves and a bulk facility to be added.

Unknown to Houston, technology would yet again bring about changes to shipping that were as profound as those generated by steam propulsion in the early 19th century, by iron and steel construction in the late 19th century, and by petroleum in the early 20th century. Change arrived at Houston in the improbable form of a converted World War II–era tanker.

In its heyday, when it was headquartered in Galveston, and later, Houston, Lykes Line was one of the largest shipping lines in the world. The Lykes Line ships in this picture can be identified by the diamond with an L in it on the funnel or the words "Lykes Line" on the hull. They are, from left to right, *Brinton Lykes*, *Elizabeth Lykes*, *Frank Lykes*, and *Mayo Lykes*. (UHDL.)

A shiny new 1950 Buick Roadmaster sedan is loaded aboard MV *Pygmalion* at the Houston Wharf Company's Long Reach docks. This car is being shipped to South America. (UHDL.)

A pressure vessel is loaded on a freighter docked to the Long Reach docks. One advantage Houston had over Galveston by the 1940s was its ability to handle very heavy cargoes. (HMM.)

Steel from Antwerp, Belgium, is unloaded from the SS *Tyson Lykes* into gondola cars in 1951. (UHDL.)

A 30-ton trailer home is hoisted aboard MV *Pygmalion* for shipment to Guanta, Venezuela. *Pygmalion* carried 10 of these trailers on this 1952 voyage. (UHDL.)

There was a full house for the Long Reach docks in May 1952. Located in the Turning Basin, this facility was the heart of the Port of Houston in the 1950s. (UHDL.)

Here, a cargo of bulk barite ore is being unloaded ore from *Axel Carl* to Texas & Pacific hoppers in 1953. Shipped from Nova Scotia, it will be used to produce drilling fluid by Milwhite Co. in Houston. (UHDL.)

Livestock was another important cargo for the Port of Houston. Here, cattle are being loaded aboard a ship in the 1950s. (UHDL.)

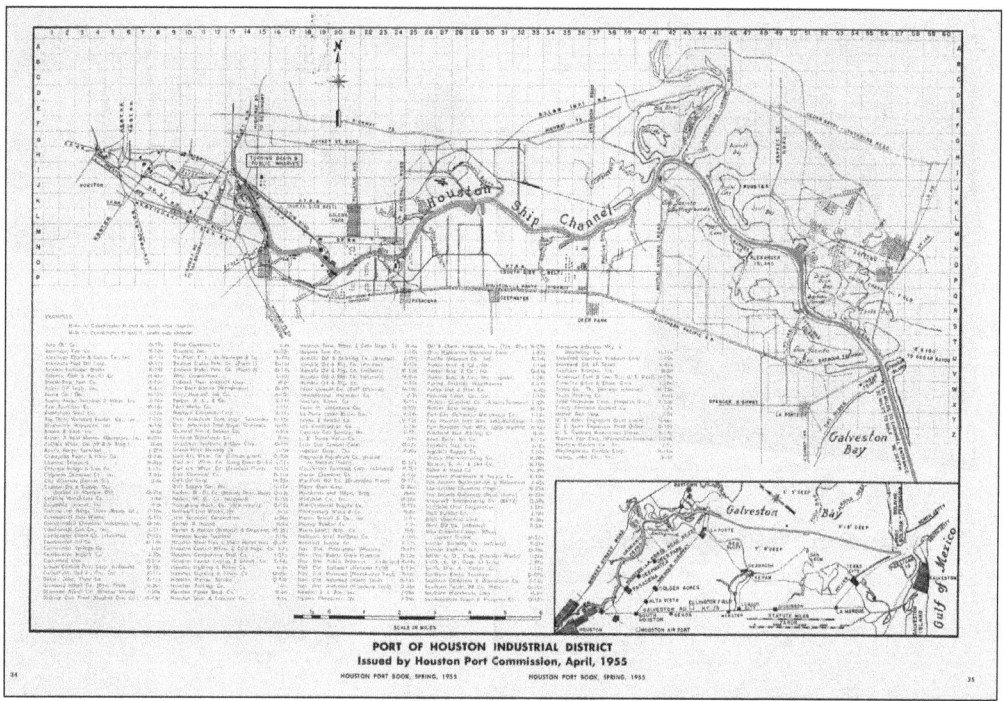

By the 1950s, the industrial district for the port stretched along 30 miles of Buffalo Bayou from the point where it reached Galveston Bay inland. (UHDL.)

Buoy tenders maintain the navigation aids along the nation's waterways. The Coast Guard buoy tender *Shadbush* was commissioned in 1944 and retired in 1976. Over its lifetime, it served at Mobile, Alabama; New Orleans, Louisiana; and along the Houston Ship Channel, based out of Galveston. (AP-HMM.)

William D. Lamport served as director of the Port of Houston from December 1953 through August 1956. (HMM.)

This photograph, taken in 1955, illustrates the partnership between the port and railroads in the shipping process, with railroad tracks leading directly into the warehouses that line the banks of the Turning Basin. (UHDL.)

The Port of Houston's public grain elevator in 1956 was a busy facility. By the 1950s, the port was shipping over 100 million bushels of grain annually. (UHDL.)

Bagged green coffee is unloaded from the SS *Rio Orinoco* in 1955. (UHDL.)

Ships line the wharves along the Turning Basin in 1956. Days like this one, when every berth was taken, motivated expansion of the port in the 1960s. (UHDL.)

Flour bound for South America is being loaded aboard the SS *Gulf Banker* at the Port of Houston while a radio crew from *Voice of America* records the event for a Latin American broadcast in 1954. (HMM.)

Steel pipe from Lone Star Steel's East Texas mill is loaded aboard the Lykes Line SS *Solon Turman* for shipment to San Juan, Puerto Rico, in May 1951. This is part of a 982-ton shipment of pipe. (UHDL.)

The Port of Houston could handle large, awkward cargoes, such as this steel truss being loaded aboard a general-cargo steamship in 1951. (UHDL.)

US flag freighter *Nishmaha* loads rebar at the Port of Houston in the 1950s. (HMM.)

Break-bulk cargo is loaded aboard a Lykes Line ship in the 1950s. Crates, bales, bags, and barrels were the standard means of shipping cargo in the 1950s. (UHDL.)

A busy dockyard scene at the Port of Houston in the 1950s shows the labor-intensive nature of handling break-bulk cargo. (HMM.)

A forklift shifts cargo in a Port of Houston warehouse in the 1950s. Cargo handling during that decade used more mechanization than it had previously, but it was still labor-intensive and time-consuming. (UHDL.)

This painting provides an idealized view of the Port of Houston at the end of the 1950s: brawny men loading bales, bags, barrels; and crates of cargo aboard streamlined, break-bulk general-cargo ships. This painting hung for years in the saloon of the inspection boat *Sam Houston*. (AP.)

Seven

The Container Revolution

When *Ideal-X* entered the Port of Houston on April 23, 1956, no one realized its cargo would change the world, revolutionize shipping, and create today's global economy. The ship was a tanker, modified to carry a deck cargo of 58 boxes that fit on a standard flatbed truck trailer.

The concept was the brainchild of Malcolm McLean. McLean owned one of the largest trucking companies in the United States and was seeking a way to speed delivery of cargo while reducing shipping cost. Initially, he shipped vans intact, but the wheels and chassis consumed too much space. Removing these, he developed a detachable box that could be locked onto the bed of a trailer, reinforced so they could be stacked.

McLean viewed the experiment a success. In 1957, his Pan-Atlantic Steamship Company initiated sea-land service offering scheduled container service. Soon, Pan-Atlantic advertised "two sailings weekly between Houston and New York [and] weekly service between Houston, Tampa, and Miami."

The description of Pan-Atlantic Sea-Land Service in the winter 1957–1958 *Houston Port Book* reads, "Operates truck terminal, handling special type trailer bodies, shipped fully loaded on trailer ships in coastwise service to Atlantic seaboard." No one, including the Port of Houston, appreciated how revolutionary McLean's innovation was.

As the 1950s closed, attention focused on space and the atom. About the same time as *Ideal-X* arrived at Houston, the US government was planning the first nuclear-powered cargo ship. The result would be NSS *Savannah*, a gorgeous clipper-bowed, mixed-cargo-passenger break-bulk vessel launched in 1959.

Galveston bet *Savannah* represented the future; an opportunity to reestablish port preeminence over Houston. Todd Shipyard in Galveston built a facility to refuel nuclear cargo ships. It seemed logical. Steamships had revolutionized trade in the early 1800s, and triple-expansion steam engines and steam turbines revolutionized shipping in the late 1800s and early 1900s. Converting fuel from coal to oil also created big changes. Fleets of commercial nuclear ships might soon be flocking to Galveston.

Fewer than a dozen commercial nuclear ships were eventually constructed. Nuclear power was only marginally better than oil and entailed headaches unforeseen in the heady 1950s. *Savannah*, the only ship to use Galveston's refueling facility, fell victim to transatlantic jet service, which siphoned off passengers and containerization and made break-bulk cargo obsolete.

Houston bet on space. The Manned Spacecraft Center arrived in Houston in 1962, in part because Houston was a port. The center even built a barge dock for maritime deliveries. A channel cut from the Houston Ship Channel through Clear Lake provided access. The port expected big things from its new neighbor.

While Florida's Kennedy Space Center—with its launch pads—needed port facilities to receive boosters, Johnson Space Center (as the space center was later renamed) proved just another industrial customer. Seagoing cargoes arrived at existing Port of Houston facilities and were trucked to the space center. Its barge dock went unused.

In the meantime, McLean's containers reshaped the port. Sea-land service exploded, and in 1960, the line renamed itself Sea-Land. Initially converting existing tankers to hold containers, by 1964 it began ordering new ships, designed from the keel up for containers. Many of those ships stopped at Houston, whose central location allowed the road—and later, the railroad—network to disburse containers quickly.

Soon, other shippers initiated container service, and the port began capitalizing on containers. The early 1960s saw the port touting the first arrival by container of different types of cargo: the first shipment of grocery supplies from Europe was in 1965; the first shipment of Germany wine was in 1967.

It also built facilities for loading and unloading containers. A 27-ton container crane was completed in 1966. Others followed. The pace of containerization quickened as other ports began adding container facilities, and many of these ports sent delegations to Houston to learn how it was done.

In retrospect, it is obvious why containerization was so successful. It slashed port costs, reducing labor required to load and unload ships. Since containers could be carried by ships, trucks, and trains, the system also cut costs throughout the shipping cycle. Cargo was packed once at its initial departure point and was unloaded once at the ultimate destination.

There were other savings, too. A locked container protected cargo from both damage and pilferage, reducing shrinkage costs. Sealing a container cut customs inspections. Moreover, containers drastically reduced loading times. With the right cargo-handling equipment, a container ship could be emptied and filled again in less than a day. Reduced idle time allowed ships to transport much more cargo annually. McLean estimated that containerization cut shipping costs by over 97 percent. No shipper could ignore that bottom line. By 1980, the traditional break-bulk cargo ship was as obsolete as sailing-era tea clippers.

The container revolution created its own language. Traffic was measured in TEUs, or twenty-foot equivalent units. The TEU represented the volume of a standard 20-foot-long shipping container.

The greatest efficiencies were achieved at ports optimized for containers. Since Houston was one of the first container ports, it was an early winner. As Houston realized the impact of containerization, it used this early lead to its best advantage, adding equipment to handle containers. In 1970, it took the radical step of planning a container-only facility. Equally radical, it opted for a new location outside the Turning Basin, building at Barbour's Cut at Morgan's Point, near the mouth of Galveston Bay. The terminal opened in 1977, the first port in Texas designed to handle standardized shipping containers.

Barbour's Cut was only one of several major expansions at the Port of Houston in the 1960s and 1970s. The bulk facility authorized in 1957 was completed in 1961. Nine miles downstream from the Turning Basin at Green's Bayou, it was the first of several new terminals built outside the traditional location of the Port of Houston. Highly automated for its day, it accelerated the trend of replacing muscle with machinery.

Another major terminal that came into existence during this period was the privately built Jacintoport Terminal. Located at the site of the old San Jacinto Ordnance Depot, it was acquired in 1964 and converted into an industrial park and terminal. As a mixed facility, it could handle general cargoes, grain, and petroleum products. It, too, was downstream of the Turning Basin, opposite the San Jacinto Battlefield Park.

The period was one of unprecedented growth for the port. Cargo tonnage stood at 60 million in 1959 and bounced between 55 and 62 million throughout the 1960s. Fueled by container traffic, oil imports, and additional cargoes shipped through the bulk cargo and other facilities added during the 1960s and 1970s, port tonnage exceeded 122,000 in 1979. Container traffic, a minor factor in 1960, had grown to over 300,000 TEUs in 1980. Along the way, the Houston Ship Channel was deepened yet again to 42 feet at Barbour's Cut.

The *Ideal-X* was a tanker built during World War II. Malcolm McLean modified it to carry a deck-load cargo of shipping containers. On April 26, 1956, *Ideal-X* left Newark, New Jersey, with 58 containers aboard. When it arrived at Houston five days later, it delivered the first load of shipping containers. (POHA.)

Ships crowd the Houston Ship Channel in 1962, six years after the arrival of the *Ideal-X* heralded the container revolution. Most are still break-bulk general-cargo vessels, but all will be retired or converted within 10 years. (UHDL.)

Break-bulk persisted into the early 1960s. Except for the mechanization provided by the forklift, this scene of bags being unloaded from a cargo ship is virtually identical to a scene from the 1920s. (UHDL.)

This 1962 view of the Port of Houston was taken from the port's observation platform. The public grain elevator can be seen in the background. (UHDL.)

Just 20 years earlier, the United States had been at war with Japan. In 1962, Houston was a regular destination for Japanese merchant ships, like this one—which traveled through the Panama Canal to reach Houston from Japan. (UHDL.)

In this busy scene at the Long Reach docks in the 1960s, palletized cargo is being lifted into break-bulk freighters. (UHDL.)

Here, bales of cotton are being loaded aboard the *Kiyosumi Maru* in 1962. Many of the bales appear to have been moved from the railroad car on handcarts. Over the next decade, Japan would embrace containerization, sending delegations to the Port of Houston to learn how it was done. (UHDL.)

Lead buttons from Australia are unloaded off the SS *Pioneer Reef* en route to the Ethyl Corporation in Pasadena, Texas, in 1961. This cargo was likely intended to create antiknock tetraethyl lead gasoline additive, which was then still legal. (UHDL.)

While Houston developed container facilities, downriver rival Galveston bet on nuclear power and built a facility to refuel nuclear cargo ships. It only serviced the NS *Savannah*, the only nuclear-powered civilian ship in US registry. (NARA.)

The Johnson Space Center (JSC) opened in Houston in 1962. While space was the final frontier, a major reason that Houston was chosen was the sea. The requirements for the space center specified it was to be located at a port, in a location that could accommodate a dock. (NASA.)

While this barge dock at JSC anchored the space center to Houston, it has only been used twice by NASA: once in the 1980s, when a Saturn V was moved to JSC for display, and once in 2012, when a shuttle mock-up was transported to JSC. (AP.)

A steam boiler is loaded aboard a ship for transport to Taiwan in 1964. The port routinely handled cargoes that were large, heavy, and delicate. (UHDL.)

While the advantage of containerization was obvious, the standardized container was a product of evolution. Other configurations appeared during the early years of the container revolution. This picture shows one early container being hoisted aboard a ship at the Port of Houston in the early 1960s. (UHDL.)

Built in 1977, Barbour's Cut terminal was the first facility constructed from the ground up at the Port of Houston as a container facility. Located below Morgan's Point, it significantly reduces the time required to dock at the Port of Houston. (ACOE.)

This is a container-handling facility at the Port of Houston. These gantry cranes, called Transtainers, allow container ships to be loaded or unloaded in hours, rather than weeks. (LOC.)

Like building blocks for a giant's child, these shipping containers fill the storage area at the Barbour's Cut facility as they await shipment to their ultimate destinations. (POHA.)

Break-bulk cargo still exists today, but most items shipped this way now are too large to fit into a cargo container, like as these wind turbine blades being unloaded at the Port of Houston for overland shipment to a Texas wind farm. (POHA.)

Containers were so successful because they were intermodal. They could go straight from a ship to a railroad flatcar or flatbed truck without requiring that anything but the container be moved. The trend accelerated in 1981 when Sea-Land stacked containers two-high on railcars at the Port of Houston, doubling the capacity a single car could carry. (HMM.)

By 1980 there were clear winners and losers in the transportation revolution sparked by the shipping container. Losers included break-bulk cargo ships and nuclear power. The clear winner was the modern container ship, such as Mediterranean Shipping Company's *Rania*, shown approaching the Port of Houston. (POHA.)

The Bulk Materials Handling Plant at Greens Bayou opened in 1962 and is capable of handling virtually any kind of dry-bulk commodity. (POHA.)

Eight
EXPANSION AND GROWTH

The Port of Houston over the final two decades of the 20th century was much different than it had been at the start of the container revolution. In many ways, it bore as much resemblance to the port of the 1950s as the port of the 1950s did to the port that existed at the dedication of the Houston Ship Channel in 1914.

Gone were teams of longshoremen muscling cargo by hand; they had been replaced by automated loading systems and crane operators. The port that stretched from the Turning Basin to the distant Manchester Terminal had leapfrogged downstream. While the Turning Basin would remain a vital part of the port, it was no longer the focus. Future growth there was constrained.

Not only was the area built out, in 1973 a bridge spanning Buffalo Bayou was built two miles downstream of the Turning Basin by the Texas Department of Transportation. Part of the Interstate 610 Loop project, it had a clearance of only 135 feet and a span of 600 feet. Port officials protested, but transportation officials ignored them.

A tight fit even in 1973, it limited the ships that could reach the Turning Basin as ships kept growing in size. As the port entered the 1980s, the Army Corps of Engineers was in the middle of planning a deepening project. The goal was to dredge the channel to 50 feet. The bridge, an impressive landmark, meant that the Turning Basin would miss out on the opportunities offered by making the port accessible to larger ships.

Deepening the Houston Ship Channel was a project initially authorized in 1968. By 1985, the channel was at least 40 feet deep and 400 feet wide, although it was deeper at other spots, such as the 42-foot depth at Barbour's Cut. The 1968 plan had called for the channel to be deepened to 45 feet, and port interests were frustrated at the slow progress. Local studies done in the mid-1980s called for the channel to be deepened to 45 feet and widened to 530 feet throughout its length, with some spots widened to a 600-foot breadth. In 1989, voters authorized bonds to pay for these improvements, although the work was not completed until 1998.

One victim of the deepening project was the Bayport Tunnel. Finished in 1953, it had a depth clearance of only 40 feet. In 1986, construction began on an eight-lane highway bridge over the Houston Ship Channel as a replacement. The Fred Hartman Bridge, completed in 1995, had a clearance of 178 feet and a span of 1,250 feet. This was sufficient not just for near-term shipping, but allowed for future growth. The Baytown Tunnel was closed in 1995 and demolished in 1997.

A third bridge over the channel, the Sam Houston Ship Channel Bridge, had been completed in 1982 eight miles downstream of the Sidney Sherman Bridge. Its height was satisfactory, providing a clearance of 175 feet, but its maximum span, 750 feet, limits widening of the channel.

The number of Port of Houston terminals increased throughout the 1980s and 1990s, as did the wharves and cargo-handling facilities at existing terminals. Barbour's Cut expanded its four container berths to six in the 1980s.

The Port of Houston Authority also acquired existing facilities along the Houston Ship Channel. In 1987, the port authority purchased the Jacintoport facility. This gave it another facility well down the channel from the Turning Basin. In 1993, two years after the Woodhouse Corporation went into bankruptcy, the port purchased that corporation's Woodhouse Terminal in Galena Park.

The port authority's purchase included the granary facility at Woodhouse. The facility was only a little bigger than the public elevator in the Turning Basin, but it had been built in 1979, over 50 years after the Turning Basin's elevator was completed. Additionally, it was downstream of the Interstate 610 bridge, which allowed access for larger vessels. The new facility was named Public Elevator No. 2. The old elevator, unable to compete with the new one in speed or berthing size, closed the next year, further reducing the influence of the Turning Basin.

Another bankruptcy made CARE Shipping's privately owned terminal in Channelview, Texas, available. Built in the late 1980s, it was then one of the most modern facilities on the Houston Ship Channel. Sensing an opportunity, the Port of Houston purchased it in 1995.

The increasing size of the port, as well as the increased volume of traffic, forced the port to reappraise its fire-protection services. In 1973, the port had added a second fireboat, *W.L. Farnsworth*, to reinforce the 1950 boat *Capt. Crotty*. Two fireboats were believed insufficient by 1980, and in 1983 *Capt. Crotty* was retired and two new fireboats—*J.C. Bracewell* and *Howard T. Tellepson*—were added. The two new boats each carried 1,000 gallons of foam. Capable of reaching 20 knots, they were equipped with three nozzles that allowed a boat to pump 2,000 gallons of water per minute. *Bracewell* was stationed in the Turning Basin, *Farnsworth*, at the Green's Bayou Bulk Facility, and *Tellepson* covered Barbour's Cut.

Cargo tonnage remained relatively flat between 1980 and 1990, growing five million tons from 1980 (120 million) to 1990 (125 million). It is a tribute to the volume of cargo handled, that five million tons, a tonnage in excess of the annual tonnage of the Port of Houston in 1923, could be considered relatively small. Tonnage growth took off in the 1990s, however, and it exceeded 148 million in 1996 and touched 175 million by 2000.

Much of that growth was due to container traffic, which increased over the 1980s. Starting at 300,000 TEUs in 1980, it touched 500,000 TEUs annually over the course of the decade. By the end of the final decade of the 20th century, it doubled again. In 2000, container shipping at port facilities exceeded one million TEUs. Changing attitudes toward container cargo helped fuel that growth. In the 1960s, containers were used for express cargoes, the seagoing equivalent of airmail. Shipping by container was so cheap that by 1990 it was being used for anything and everything.

The Sydney Sherman Bridge is known popularly as the "Ship Channel Bridge." Its main span is 600 feet wide and has a clearance of 135 feet, providing a challenge to ships passing under it. It has been struck several times (LOC.)

Keeping the Houston Ship Channel navigable is an ongoing task, and several pipeline dredges are employed to maintain the depth and width of the channel and prevent it from filling in. (POHA.)

Here is the Houston Ship Channel as seen from space in the late 20th century. This view shows the stretch between the Interstate 610 bridge and the San Jacinto Monument and illustrates the density of petrochemical and industrial facilities along that part of the channel. (NASA.)

Refineries continued to play an important role at the Port of Houston in the 1980s and 1990s. Many, such as this one, had been operating on the Houston Ship Channel for over 50 years. (AP.)

By the late 20th century, both sides of the channel at the Turning Basin are developed, with warehouses and cargo facilities lining the banks. This photograph shows the size of the industrial area that had been established around the port by the 1990s. (LOC.)

An aerial view of the Houston Ship Channel just to the east of the Turning Basin in the late 20th century shows the variety of cargoes the port handles. The bulk carrier anchored on the north bank of the channel has a deck cargo of yachts. (LOC.)

J.S. Bracewell is one of three fireboats in the Port of Houston's fire department. Launched in 1983, it is still in use today. It can pump between 4,000 to 6,000 gallons per minute. (POHA.)

Public Elevator No. 1, located at the Turning Basin, was an important part of the port through much of the 20th century. It was shut down after the port acquired Public Elevator No. 2 in 1992. (AP.)

Public Elevator No. 2, in Galena Park, was built in 1979 and acquired by the Port of Houston in 1992 as part of the purchase of the Woodhouse Terminal. It can store of 6.2 million bushels of grain and can load 120,000 bushels per hour. (AP.)

A petroleum terminal on the Houston Ship Channel near the Galveston Bay receives a cargo of crude oil from a docked tanker. (LOC.)

The San Jacinto Monument is a notable landmark along the Houston Ship Channel. The Jacintoport facility is on the far side of the channel, across from the monument. (LOC.)

The Woodhouse Terminal, located near Sims Bayou, has the deepest draft (39 feet) of any Port of Houston wharf. A general-cargo facility, it was acquired in 1998 as part of the port's expansion for the 21st century. (POHA.)

In addition to the commercial and industrial uses of the Houston Ship Channel and Port of Houston, recreational use of the water has soared. The channel can be seen as it passes through Galveston Bay behind this marina in Clear Lake (LOC.)

Pictured here is one of the oil terminals at the Port of Houston. By tonnage, petroleum and petroleum products ranked first among imports and second among exports for the port during the 1980s and 1990s. (LOC.)

Although most recent construction has occurred downstream, the Turning Basin remains a vital part of the port. The region near the Turning Basin is filled with ships on a typical day in the late 20th century. (A.P.)

Barge traffic has been an important part of the port's activities since the inception of the port and remains important today. Barges are an energy-efficient way to move bulk cargos. (A.P.)

This is the Houston Lighting & Power Deepwater Plant as it appeared in the late 1990s prior to the demolition of the original power plant. It has been a Houston Ship Channel landmark since the 1920s. (AP.)

Built in 1982 and named for a director at the Port of Houston, tugboat *Vernon Bailey* has been a familiar sight along the Houston Ship Channel for over three decades. (AP.)

While the Port of Houston has always depended upon rail transportation for its cargoes, trains have had an even greater role since the introduction of the standard shipping container in the 1970s, and local rail yards link the port with inland regions. (LOC.)

A container ship unloads cargo from at the Port of Houston gantry just west of the Sidney Sherman Bridge. Trucks wait to receive the containers on shore next to the ship. (AP.)

Nine

A 21st-Century Port

The Port of Houston continues to grow. As much tonnage now moves through the Houston Ship Channel annually as moved through the port in its first quarter century following completion of the channel in 1914. In 2010, the port handled 225 million tons of cargo. Ship arrivals topped 7,700, and 150,000 barges used the port that year. In 2012, the port, directly or indirectly, created 1,026,820 jobs and $178.5 billion in economic impact. This is dramatically up from 785,000 jobs and $118 billion impact that a 2007 survey reported. In 2012, the Port of Houston handled nearly 1.2 million containers, or 1.9 million TEUs, carried by 8,395 vessels. By its centennial in 2014, it should exceed two million TEUs.

The Port of Houston is now ranked second in total tonnage for ports in the United States. Ranked first is the Port of South Louisiana, located on a stretch of the Mississippi River between New Orleans and Baton Rouge. Its tonnage benefits from Mississippi barges loading oceangoing ships, allowing it to count the same tonnage twice. Houston is ranked first among US ports in foreign tonnage and is seventh in container tonnage (as measured in TEUs). It is Texas's largest port, with a 46 percent market share. Two-thirds of all containers that use Gulf Coast ports go through the Port of Houston, and 98 percent of containers using Texas ports pass through the Port of Houston.

Despite success, the Port of Houston faces new challenges as a 21st-century port.

The increasing volume of container traffic is one. By the start of this century, the Barbour's Cut facility was working at capacity and had no room for further expansion. In response, the Port of Houston planned and built a second container terminal, the Bayport Container Terminal. Opened in 2007, the new facility represented another step in the port's march to the Gulf of Mexico. Located on Galveston Bay between Barbour's Cut and Clear Lake, it has the capacity to handle 2.3 million TEUs annually, more than the total the entire port currently receives.

Nor is the head of navigation being neglected. Realizing the limitations of the Turning Basin, the port approved a major improvement of that terminal in 2012. Many of the terminal's buildings date to the 1920s, and these old, obsolete buildings will be razed and replaced by state-of-the-art facilities. The port plans to invest $14 million in this renovation. It also invited the Houston Maritime Museum, founded in 2000 and located in the museum district, to relocate to the Turning Basin.

Another challenge is port security. Before the attacks of September 11, 2001, port officials thought about port security in terms of dockside theft of cargo and drug smuggling. Today, port officials have to worry about terrorism and human trafficking. Port facilities and Houston Ship Channel industries potentially offer attractive targets and could also serve as a conduit for both illegal aliens and terrorist traffic. A container could easily contain a nuclear device or be converted into living quarters for those seeking to enter the United States without clearing customs.

In response, the port has upgraded security in many ways. The days of casual employment as a longshoreman are now history. Anyone working within the port now needs a Transportation

Worker Identification Credential (TWIC) issued by the federal government. The card requires a background check and must be renewed periodically.

Coast Guard presence has been beefed up, with a new emphasis on antiterrorism. Customs screening has also improved, and sensors screen cargoes for explosives or radiation emissions. The port has upgraded it surveillance systems and installed a state-of-the-art security headquarters that allows better integration of security information, facilitates coordination between different law-enforcement agencies, and permits faster response to emerging situations.

Environmental concerns are also being addressed during the 21st century. The area of the Houston Ship Channel and the Port of Houston is more than just an industrial region; it is a major wetland. The Port of Houston takes environmental stewardship seriously, and in 2002 it was the first US port to achieve certification under ISO 14001, the international standard for environmental-management systems, and it has maintained certification since then. The Bayport Terminal, when constructed, was built with environmental principles in mind. The administration building was constructed to Leadership in Energy and Environmental Design (LEED) standards.

Another challenge is being presented by the Panama Canal expansion. New, larger locks will provide access between the Gulf of Mexico and the Pacific to much larger ships, increasing maximum sizes from 950 feet by 106 feet by 39.5 feet to 1,400 feet by 180 feet by 60 feet. When completed, the locks will triple the cargo capacity of the Panama Canal. The most significant factor is the new 60-foot-maximum draft. The Houston Ship Channel currently has a depth of only 45 feet, and the channels to the Bayport and Barbour's Cut Terminal are less than that.

Initially, the port plans to deepen the channels to its two container terminals to 45 feet. However, as container ships increase in size to use the capacity offered by the Panama Canal, the Port of Houston will have two choices. It can either deepen the channel to at least 60 feet, or it can watch the biggest container ships use a different port. Plans have studied the possibility of having the Houston Ship Channel dredged to 60 feet from Bolivar Roads to the Turning Basin, but this seems unlikely to happen, at least initially. Another possible plan would see the ship channel dredged to a 98-foot depth from Bolivar Roads to the Bayport Container Facility, which is about 30 miles from the Turning Basin. If the choice is surrendering preeminence as a container-shipping port, increasing the channel's depth to 60 feet, or to 98 feet, to at least one of its major container terminals will become a priority.

The future holds only one certainty for the Port of Houston: change. Steamboats in the 1830s, to iron ships in the 1890s, long-haul trucking in the 1930s, and containers in the 1960s have all changed the port in unanticipated ways, as has man's ability to transform the landscape through dredging and building. When technology and geography intersect, the results can be unexpected.

Barbour's Cut was the first container facility built for the Port of Houston. Although it has been supplemented by the Bayport Container Terminal, it remains a vital part of the port for the next century. (POHA.)

Opened in 2007, the Bayport Container Terminal is the Port of Houston's newest container facility. Located between La Porte and Seabrook, Texas, it was built to expand the port's container capacity when Barbour's Cut could no longer be expanded. (POHA.)

An aerial view of the Bayport Container Terminal shows the size of the facility. It has 376 acres of container yard and a 123-acre intermodal facility. (POHA.)

The Turning Basin in the 21st century retains many of the warehouses erected during the 1920s. The port plans to replace these with state-of-the-art facilities. (POHA.)

The Turning Basin is the oldest active part of the Port of Houston, but it remains important and will continue to serve the port as it enters its second century. (POHA.)

The Jacintoport Terminal is located on the north side of the Houston Ship Channel near Channelview, Texas. It is one of the Port of Houston's general-cargo facilities, capable of handling a wide range of cargoes. It includes a bagged-cargo–handling system. (POHA.)

Security has become an important concern for the Port of Houston since September 11, 2001. Possession of a transportation worker's identification credential is now required for access to many parts of the port. (POHA.)

The Port of Houston maintains its own police force and uses state-of-the-art technology to monitor activities within the port. (POHA.)

To improve port security in a post–September 11 age, the US Coast Guard stands watch over the Port of Houston and Houston Ship Channel from its Coast Guard Wharf in Galena Park, Texas. (AP.)

The Houston Ship Channel is a wildlife area as well as an industrial district. The intertidal marshes that line the channel provide a home to a wealth of birds, amphibians, reptiles, and mammals. (ACOE.)

Today, the Port of Houston is as concerned about the environment as it is about the economy. This volunteer is planting sea grass near the Houston Ship Channel in coordination with the Galveston District of the Army Corps of Engineers. (ACOE.)

Crude-oil tanker *Aegean Glory* unloads its cargo at a Port of Houston facility. Petroleum remains a major cargo at the port in the 21st century. (POHA.)

A bulk carrier awaits cargo at the Port of Houston's Public Elevator No. 2. In the 21st century, this facility has regularly processed over two million tons of grain annually. (POHA.)

While containers have grown in importance, the port's ability to handle outsize and heavy cargoes remains one reason shippers still use it. Here, steel pipe is unloaded. (POHA.)

The *Stolt Quetzal*, a chemical tanker built in 2009 for Stolt-Nielsen, is one of the many tankers using the Port of Houston in the 21st century. (POHA.)

Panama began an expansion of its canal in 2007. The increased size of the locks will create new challenges and opportunities for the Port of Houston as great as those that accompanied the original completion of the Panama Canal in 1914. (Photograph courtesy of William Lardas.)

With the increase in the size of the Panama Canal, the Port of Houston is responding to the opportunity offered with plans to deepen the Houston Ship Channel to a 98-foot depth using dredges like this one. (POHA.)

In the 19th century, the banks of Buffalo Bayou near the foot of Main Street were lined with manufacturing buildings, warehouses, and industrial docks. Today, the banks of this part of Buffalo Bayou are a park, used more by joggers than by steamboat men. (LOC.)

This is Allens' Landing—or a reasonable facsimile—as it appears today. Because of changes in the bed of Buffalo Bayou, the actual location of the original Allen's Landing is unknown. This image captures the narrowness of the river at that point. (AP.)

BIBLIOGRAPHY

Alperin, Lynn M. *Custodians of the Coast: History of the United States Army Engineers at Galveston.* Galveston, TX: Galveston District, US Army Corps of Engineers, 1977.

Hall, Andrew W. *The Galveston-Houston Packet: Steamboats on Buffalo Bayou.* Charleston, SC: History Press, 2012.

Sibley, Marilyn McAdams. *The Port of Houston: A History.* Austin: University of Texas Press, 1968.

Trimble, Frances G. *The Houston Pilots: Silent Servants of Progress.* Houston: Houston Pilots, 2004.

Vela, Lee and Maxine Edwards. *Reaching for the Sea: The Story of the Port of Houston on Its 75th Anniversary.* Houston: Port of Houston Authority, 1989.

www.portarchive.com.

Visit us at
arcadiapublishing.com

www.ingramcontent.com/pod-product-compliance
Lightning Source LLC
Chambersburg PA
CBHW050657150426
42813CB00055B/2215